The Invisible among Us

"As we journey on the Pilgrimage of Justice and
Peace, *The Invisible among Us* is a reminder for the
Christian family to bring to the centre those who
are left on the margins, are forgotten and rendered
'legally invisible.'"

– Rev. Dr Cornelia Füllkrug-Weitzel
President, Brot für die Welt / Bread for the World

GW00566731

Visions & Voices
Personal Perspectives on Justice and Peace

Life itself is endangered today. Yet Christians around the world have vital insights, convictions, and traditions to engage positively in fostering life, confronting cultures and practices of death, and building justice and peace.

Exploring many of the issues raised by the theme "God of Life, lead us to justice and peace," this series offers brief volumes from leading Christian thinkers and activists. Centred on the four arenas of Just Peace (peoples, community, marketplace, and the earth), the books present strong opinions forcefully argued on many of the most pressing and important issues of our day. Initial volumes include

Clare Amos
Peace-ing Together Jerusalem

Edward Dommen
A Peaceable Economy

Meehyun Chung
Liberation and Reconciliation

Jessie Fubara-Manuel
Giver of Life, Hear Our Cries!

Tatha Wiley
Misusing Sin

Donald Eugene Miller
From Just War to Just Peace

The Invisible among Us
Hidden, Forgotten, Stateless

Semegnish Asfaw

World Council of Churches Publications

THE INVISIBLE AMONG US
Hidden, Forgotten, Stateless
Semegnish Asfaw

WCC Publications is the book publishing programme of the World Council of Churches. Founded in 1948, the WCC promotes Christian unity in faith, witness, and service for a just and peaceful world. A global fellowship, the WCC brings together more than 345 Protestant, Orthodox, Anglican, and other churches representing more than 550 million Christians in 110 countries and works cooperatively with the Roman Catholic Church.

Opinions expressed in WCC Publications are those of the authors.

Scripture quotations are from the New Revised Standard Version Bible, © copyright 1989 by the Division of Christian Education of the National Council of the Churches of Christ in the USA. Used by permission.

Cover design: Julie Kauffman Design
Cover image: *Three People Walking* ©Antoinettew|Dreamstime.com
Interior design and typesetting: Julie Kauffman Design

ISBN: 978-2-8254-1684-6
World Council of Churches
150 route de Ferney, P.O. Box 2100
1211 Geneva 2, Switzerland
http://publications.oikoumene.org

CONTENTS

For my late father
For my mother, brothers, and sister
For my husband, Antoine
For my friends, who supported this project
With gratitude

Some of them have left behind a name,
so that others declare their praise.
But of others there is no memory;
they have perished as though they had never existed;
they have become as though they had never been born,
they and their children after them.
– Sirach 44: 8-9

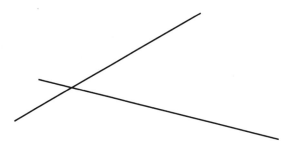

Preface

Nationality is the legal link between an individual and a state. It is an element of membership, of belongingness to a group, a nation, a state. Recognized as a fundamental right by Article 15 of the Universal Declaration on Human Rights (UDHR), it is a right to which all human beings are entitled by virtue of being part of the human family.

Statelessness is the antonym of nationality: it is the absence of nationality, of this legal link proving our membership to a state. Not being recognized as citizens by any state, stateless persons do not benefit from the protection of any state. Statelessness is an anomaly of the modern state system and of the international legal framework developed over the last seven decades. It is about being vulnerable, defenceless. Since they do not legally exist, stateless people are "invisible" to the state system, hidden, marginalized, forgotten, yet living in our midst. *Invisible among us.*

Stateless persons are deprived of the fundamental right to be full members of the society in which they were born and are living. Just like any other human being, they aspire for recognition, for a place in the world, in the community of beings. They yearn to be accepted and be part of a community, a history, a country. For without citizenship, they are often unable to have access to health care, get a decent education, vote, travel freely, find accommodation, open a bank account, own property, etc. All these aspects of life that nationals often take for granted are inaccessible and out of reach for stateless persons.

In the face of increasing security concerns that have affected several Western countries in the last years, deprivation of nationality has been a topical and controversial issue, for instance prompting the resignation in early 2016 of Christiane Taubira from her position as France's Minister of Justice, as a sign of protest to the French government's intention to amend its constitution in order to strip French bi-nationals accused of terrorist acts of their French nationality. France is not an isolated case: several other countries have also been considering deprivation of nationality as a tool in responding to such security threats.

The World Council of Churches (WCC), through its Commission of the Churches on International Affairs (CCIA), has a long tradition of upholding and defending human rights for all, especially for those who are marginalized and rendered voiceless. The plight of stateless persons, and the lack of attention they receive, are no exceptions to this tradition.

During its 50th meeting in September 2010 in Albania, the CCIA was given the mandate to take up the issue of statelessness as one of its advocacy focuses. Much has been achieved since then, including solidarity visits to stateless communities in Bangladesh and Nepal followed by a regional consultation in Dhaka (December 2011), as well as a major international conference in Washington DC (February 2013).

The process led to the first WCC statement on the human rights of stateless people adopted during the WCC 10th Assembly in Busan, Republic of Korea, requesting "the WCC to take up the issue of stateless people as one of its programmatic priorities until the forthcoming WCC 11th Assembly." In the spirit of the assembly mandate, the WCC/ CCIA and *Kerk in Actie* organized, a few days prior to the first Global Forum on Statelessness (The Hague, 15-17 September 2014), an international ecumenical consultation in Den Dolder. At the consultation, participants came up with a series of recommendations to help guide churches and church-related groups in action when dealing with matters of statelessness.

Statelessness as an issue is of particular pertinence to our Christian tradition: as the 10th Assembly Statement on the Human Rights of Stateless People rightly puts it,

The underlying theological assumption of active concern for those who are suffering is the belief that all people created by God constitute an inextricable unity. Solidarity and compassion are virtues that all Christians are called to practice, regardless of their possessions, as signs of their Christian discipleship. Compassion and care for one another and acknowledging the image of God in all humanity is at the core of our Christian identity and an expression of Christian discipleship. Humanitarian conduct is an essential part of the Gospel. We are instructed in Micah 6:8 to "do justice." And the commandment of love, the greatest commandment of our Lord Jesus Christ, is to love God and to love one another.

There are several causes of and consequences of statelessness, as we will see in the following chapters. In some contexts, statelessness can be the product of interrelated causes, thus calling for a holistic and comprehensive response. It is therefore helpful to collaborate with the United Nations High Commission for Refugees (UNHCR) and other United Nations (UN) bodies, faith-based organizations, civil society, and all relevant stakeholders in order to achieve a meaningful and sustainable impact.

Depending on their local realities, churches and other religious communities will find the question of statelessness pertinent to their respective contexts. For instance, the issue of statelessness is of particular importance today for churches grappling with the refugee crisis from Syria and Iraq. As a result of discriminatory nationality laws that do not allow mothers to pass on their nationality to their children or even register their birth, an entire generation of children born without the presence of their father in refugee camps or on other migratory routes risks becoming stateless in the future.

WCC constituency can also get involved in the issue of statelessness, for instance by protecting stateless persons and making sure their basic rights are respected, or by preventing new cases of statelessness from arising in order to reduce vulnerabilities to exploitation, marginalization, and discrimination.

This publication is an attempt to provide an introduction and serve as a guide elaborating on basic elements of statelessness. It aims to raise awareness among the ecumenical family about some aspects of this little known problem, and to inform churches and church partners about possible avenues to prevent statelessness and protect stateless people.

The WCC 10th Assembly in Busan has invited the ecumenical family to embark on a Pilgrimage of Justice and Peace – Let us also include stateless people in this journey and build just and inclusive societies.

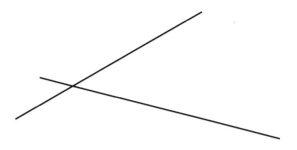

1. Who Is Stateless? Why? Where?

On April 1, 1999, an article in the *New York Times* contained the following paragraph:

> Kenneth D. Kaunda, the father of modern Zambia and the country's President for 27 years, was declared a stateless person by the country's High Court today. Ruling on a case brought by high-ranking members of the present governing party, the court ruled that Mr Kaunda is not a Zambian citizen under the Constitution because his parents were from the former British Nyasaland, now called Malawi. Mr Kaunda renounced his Malawian citizenship years ago, when he was President, so he is now effectively stateless.[1]

This excerpt is not an April's fool prank. Kenneth Kaunda, founder and president of Zambia for 27 years, was indeed declared stateless by a High Court ruling in 1999. His opponent, Frederick J. Chiluba from the Movement for Multiparty Democracy, filed a petition against him and later tried to deport him to Malawi on the grounds that his parents were born there. Former Zambian President Kaunda's lawyers appealed to the Supreme Court, and after months of his living as a stateless person, the Supreme Court finally recognized him again as a citizen of Zambia in 2000.

This widely publicized case involving a well-known political figure brought our attention to the issue of statelessness. This case also shows us that even high profile people can be affected by statelessness. Unfortunately, most of the world's stateless people do not benefit from such notoriety, and therefore their fate is completely overlooked and forgotten. Statelessness is a silent, hidden and neglected tragedy of our modern times, disrupting the existence of millions of people and impacting on the lives of these individuals, their families, and their communities. Women and children are disproportionately affected by this issue.

But what is statelessness about? Who are these stateless people? How does one technically become stateless? What are the concrete effects it has on the lives of these millions of people?

Definition and Scope of Statelessness

Most of us usually take our nationality for granted. Unless we are asked to show our passport at immigration counters when traveling, or unless we have to show an identity card in order to be able to vote, our everyday life provides us with few opportunities to reflect on and appreciate our citizenship and the countless rights derived from this status. We usually take for granted simple things of life, such as benefitting from medical care when we or our family members become ill, registering our children in schools, applying for a job, owning property, opening a bank account, or getting married. Our citizenship provides us daily with a wide range of possibilities that we naturally enjoy, without even questioning them. But what about those who are not citizens, and particularly those who are not recognized as citizens by any country?

Stateless persons, that is, individuals with no nationality, are defined in Article 1 of the 1954 Convention relating to the Status of Stateless Persons (1954 Convention) as people who are "not considered as a national by any State under the operation of its law." Stateless people have no links to any state through the legal bond of citizenship, and therefore are not recognized as citizens by any country in this world we live in. Statelessness, then, is the opposite of nationality. And so, in order to fully understand statelessness, let us first look at what nationality is and how it is acquired. The United Nations High Commission for Refugees (UNHCR) has the mandate to prevent and reduce statelessness around the world, as well as to protect the rights of stateless people. UNHCR works with governments, other UN agencies, and civil society at large in the following four areas: (1) through *identification* of stateless people, by collating information on the scope, causes, and consequences of statelessness; (2) through *prevention* of statelessness, by addressing the root causes and encouraging states to accede to the Statelessness Conventions; (3) through *reduction* of statelessness, by supporting governments to introduce changes in their laws and improving modalities to allow stateless people to acquire a nationality; and (4) through *protection* of stateless people, by making sure they are able to exercise their rights.

Nationality, the proof of membership

Nationality is a central element to the Westphalian state system we live in. It is a formal form of allegiance to a state and also confers a sense of membership and belongingness to a given state. Nationality comes with a wide range of rights that nationals can enjoy, as well as a number of duties they have to perform. For instance, citizens have the right to vote during elections or to take public office; in terms of duties, some countries require citizens to perform military service when they reach a certain age. Through the legal bond of nationality, the state also provides protection to its nationals, both within the country and outside (consular protection).

States have the primary responsibility of deciding who is a citizen and who is not. They enact the laws and define the criteria by which individuals can acquire or lose nationality. In most countries around the world, individuals become citizens of a given country either through parentage (*jus sanguinis*) or through birth place (*jus soli*), and in some cases through a combination of both.

A quick glance at the world's stateless communities

An article from the *Forced Migration Review* notes,

> The stateless typically are not free-floating, deracinated individuals, moving aimlessly around the globe. They are usually people settled in particular societies, albeit lacking legal recognition of and appropriate protection for their status as residents. The primary injustice the stateless experience, then, is not that they cannot find a state to grant them citizenship but that the state which should grant them citizenship will, for various reasons, not do so.[2]

Stateless people can be found in all continents. Statelessness affects people from all horizons and all social ranks. The anecdote that opened this chapter about former Zambian

President Kaunda is an illustration that not even high-profile persons are spared from becoming stateless.

As a result of their lack of documentation, stateless people and communities are often unknown, overlooked, "hidden." It is difficult to accurately estimate the number of stateless people worldwide either because stateless people are hiding due to fear that the state will identify and persecute them, or because states are unable (due to poor documentation systems) or reluctant to include them in the national census (due to political sensitivities). As part of its role in identifying stateless people, UNHCR is the main organization that systematically collects data on stateless people worldwide.

According to UNHCR, there are currently more than 10 million stateless people around the world. Statelessness is a global issue: to date, no region of the world has been left untouched. "Statelessness was first recognized as a global problem during the first half of the 20th century. Now it is recognized that every region of the world is not free of the problems that lead to statelessness."[3] Most of the world's stateless people can be found in Asia and Africa, as well as in the Caribbean and Europe.

In Africa, Côte d'Ivoire has the highest number of stateless persons, with an estimated 700,000 at the end of 2013 according to UNHCR. Before independence, the colonial authorities forcibly imported labour from the territory of what is now Burkina Faso. Even after independence, Côte d'Ivoire continued to welcome West African immigrants – particularly from Burkina Faso, Mali, and Ghana – who came to work on cocoa, coffee, and cotton plantations. However, since 1972, restrictive nationality rules targeting particularly descendants of emigrants have been enforced, bringing about the concept "*ivoirité*," that is, of national identity. Later on, the nationality law was changed to follow the *jus sanguinis* rule, that is, purely on descent. After the death of former President Houphouët Boigny in the mid-1990s, the country's legislations denied identification documents to all those who were perceived to be of foreign descent, thus leading to the rebellion that broke out in 2002.

The UNHCR also reports cases of statelessness in the Democratic Republic of Congo (DRC), Kenya, Madagascar, South Africa, and Zimbabwe. Unfortunately, for most of these countries, the UN agency has no clear data on the scale of the phenomenon.

UNHCR data indicate that Asia has the highest number of stateless people compared to other regions. These countries include Myanmar, Thailand, Malaysia, Vietnam, Bhutan, Nepal, and Cambodia. For instance, in Bhutan, the Lhotshampas account for more than 10 percent of the population. They are descendants of migrants of Nepali origin who came to Bhutan in the 19th century as labourers. Although they were granted Bhutanese citizenship by a 1958 Citizenship Act, a series of nationality reforms in the 1980s that retroactively applied strict criteria rendered hundreds of thousands of them stateless. The government expelled over 100,000 ethnic Nepali to Nepal, where they became stateless refugees.

In the Americas, the incidence of statelessness is lowest compared to other regions. Among countries there, Dominican Republic has the highest number of stateless people. Similar to the circumstances in Côte d'Ivoire and Bhutan, people in Dominican Republic who have been retroactively rendered stateless are descendants of migrants from Haiti who came to work in the Dominican Republic decades ago. We will discuss their situation in detail in Chapter 2.

UNHCR data for the United States and Canada indicate cases of a few hundred stateless people in each country. These are mainly individuals registered as stateless in the countries' asylum and immigration channels.

Among the millions of stateless people worldwide, UNHCR estimates that more than 680,000 live in Europe. Latvia has the highest number of stateless people in the region, representing more than 10 percent of its population. Although most Roma people in Europe have a nationality, many of them still continue to face difficulties accessing the documents necessary to confirm it.

Regarding the Middle East and North Africa, UNHCR reports cases of hundreds of thousands of stateless Bidoons in the Gulf countries. Over 200,000 Kurds in Syria and Lebanon are also stateless. In addition, throughout the entire region, including in Iraq, Lebanon, and Syria, gender-biased nationality laws do not allow women to pass on their nationality to their children

But how do individuals become stateless?

Causes of Statelessness

In our modern world, with the discourse on human rights at its height, more than ten million people are stateless and live with no legal identity. As a result, most of them are deprived of their fundamental human rights, which increases their vulnerability. Several factors cause statelessness.

We have seen that states are the primary agents responsible for assessing and defining the specific protocols for individuals to become citizens – and thereby to possess the legal bond of citizenship that links them to the state. States usually attribute nationality either based on place of birth (*jus soli*) or through descent (*jus sanguinis*). An ideal scenario is when both these rules are applied, that is, when nationality can be acquired through descent and place of birth.

The various preceding examples (Bhutan, Côte d'Ivoire, Dominican Republic) have shown us that statelessness can result from discriminatory practices targeted against specific groups in the population based on their origin or ethnicity. In these cases, statelessness resulted from strict nationality laws granting citizenship to individuals meeting specific ethnic criteria. This has resulted in the deprivation of nationality of individuals who, a few decades ago, were considered as nationals. We will see in the next chapter that stripping individuals and communities of their nationality can be used as a weapon – a tool for discriminating further and subduing a targeted group of the population.

Some states have also been considering deprivation of nationality in cases of treason, espionage, or terrorist attacks. Debates in the United Kingdom since 2010 and in France since 2015 in the aftermath of various terrorist attacks are symptomatic of measures states contemplate when they believe individuals do not fulfill criteria of allegiance to the state and its values. Such measures can lead to statelessness if the individual does not have double or multiple nationality.

Statelessness can also result from conflicts of laws and gaps in nationality laws. Let us imagine the fictitious scenario of a child being born out of wedlock in Lithuania of a Bahraini mother and a Danish father. At the age of two, the child settles in Bahrain with his or her mother. The child is stateless for a number of reasons: Danish law holds that, in cases of children born out of wedlock, nationality is granted only if the child is born in Denmark; Bahraini nationality laws do not allow women to confer nationality to their children; and Lithuanian law stipulates that in order for the child to become Lithuanian, at least one parent needs to hold that nationality. It is only after living in Bahrain for fifteen years that the child will be able to apply for Bahraini citizenship.

Twenty-seven countries in the world today do not allow women to confer nationality to their children on an equal basis with men. Gender discrimination in nationality laws can result in statelessness if the father is unable, unwilling, or not present to pass on his nationality to the child. The child will automatically be born stateless. Statelessness at birth also affects children born from stateless parents in countries that do not apply the *jus soli* rule, unless the nationality laws of the country where the child is born stipulate otherwise. In these latter cases, the child will be granted the nationality of his or her country of birth.

Linked to the issue of gender discrimination in nationality laws is the fact that in some countries women who marry a foreign national automatically lose their nationality. In case of divorce or death of the husband, the woman risks becoming stateless unless she is able to get her original nationality back.

Lack of birth registration can also put children at risk of becoming stateless. Without any official record confirming their existence, children can become stateless if they have no means of proving their nationality once they reach adulthood.

State succession and the subsequent modification of borders are other factors that can lead to statelessness. When deciding who their nationals are, newly formed states may overlook, at times deliberately, a portion of the population, thus rendering its members stateless. For instance, the dissolution of the former Soviet Union and Yugoslavia made more than half a million people stateless.

Renunciation of nationality can also be a voluntary decision taken by an individual who does not want to be the citizen of a given state and therefore refuses the state's protection. If such individuals do not have another nationality, they risk becoming stateless. For instance, German philosopher Karl Marx renounced his Prussian citizenship in 1845 and lived as a stateless person for 38 years until he died. Likewise, Friedrich Nietzsche gave up his Prussian citizenship in 1868 and remained stateless until his death in 1900. Albert Einstein also gave up his citizenship in the German Kingdom of Württemberg (to avoid military service), and was stateless from 1896 to 1901. He then became naturalized as Swiss citizen. Nowadays, states require individuals who want to renounce their nationality to show evidence that they hold – or are in the process of getting – another citizenship. If not, the individuals will become stateless.

The impact of climate change on low-lying islands such as Tuvalu and Kiribati leads some to fear that in a few decades these islands will be submerged by the rising sea level. With the absence of physical territory, will the nationals of these countries be considered stateless? There are already hundreds of climate-displaced persons coming from these low-lying islands. Do they risk becoming stateless when their islands completely

disappear? In the next section, we look at the impact statelessness has on the lives of individuals and their families – even
unto generations – as well as on entire communities.

Impact of Statelessness

To be stripped of citizenship is to be stripped of worldliness:
it is like returning to a wilderness as cavemen or savages . . .
Rightless people . . . could live and die without leaving any trace.
– Hanna Arendt, *The Origins of Totalitarianism*[4]

In practice, stateless people do not have many rights. Since no
state claims them as their citizens, they do not have the benefit of state protection. No government stands up for them.
Unless they manage to get a nationality, stateless people face a
lifetime of challenges and hardship. Statelessness affects individuals, families, communities, and generations: "The lives of
stateless people are put on 'hold' until their nationality status
can be resolved."[5] On the individual level, statelessness often
leads to a sense of disenfranchisement, worthlessness, disem-
powerment, and voicelessness. Railya, a stateless ethnic Tatar
born in Kazakhstan now living in France, compares statelessness to tumbleweed: "It rolls . . . with the breeze it rolls away.
That is what it is. That is statelessness. . . . And me, I want to
put down roots."[6]

As human beings, most of us need to feel that we are members of a nation, that we belong to a history, that we are rooted in the traditions and customs of our ancestors. We like to feel that we are contributing to the society and the country we are living in. When travelling abroad, we are proud to share about our country, our history, our values. This feeling of belongingness is rooted deep in our very being. Without any "legal" connection to any state, stateless people are denied this membership. This can lead to a lack of confidence, or to mental health issues such as depression or suicide. Stateless people feel rejected by the countries they were born in and called "home." They feel invisible, "valueless." Lack of nationality is a form of denial of their personhood and of their very existence.

Stateless people are often marginalized and discriminated against – to some extent "ostracized" – thus prolonging their economic vulnerability and the precarious conditions in which many of them live. In search of a better future, many stateless people migrate abroad or seek asylum in another country. They often have to go through irregular channels because they lack travel documents, and in doing so risk the humiliating experience of being stopped without proper identification at borders by immigration officials. They face the threat of being detained for prolonged periods in immigration centres, where they can end up trapped indefinitely because there is no country to which they can be deported.

Furthermore, stateless people often cannot own or inherit property. Property rights in many countries are often reserved for nationals. In most countries, people must have identity documents in order to buy or inherit any form of property. As a result of their inability to register any property in their name, they will lose any claim over it.

Statelessness disproportionately affects women and girls, as it increases their vulnerability to sexual and gender-based violence, exploitation, and trafficking.[7] Being legally invisible, such women become easy prey for unscrupulous traffickers who can easily smuggle them to other countries and force them to work in slavery-like conditions. Because they have no legal identity, they do not benefit from the protection of the law and are afraid to report the violence they experience, including rape. Some stateless women choose to marry in order to secure a nationality, or some kind of legal status; however, even in these cases, the women risk becoming victims of domestic violence or exploitation since they entered this relationship in a position of vulnerability.

Statelessness causes instability in a country, as it can potentially translate into unrest, population displacement, or conflict. When statelessness is used by the state as a political tool to weaken a group within its population, the stateless group becomes frustrated over time, which can lead to unrest and eventually internal strife. Nationality therefore contributes to human security.

Although matters of nationality belong primarily to states, states also have an obligation to respect international human rights law – including customary law – as well as internationally contracted agreements. The next section looks at the issue of nationality and statelessness on this broader, international stage.

The Right to a Nationality and International Human Rights Law

The human rights law framework was developed in the aftermath of the atrocities committed during the Second World War (WWII), during which national laws in some countries were manipulated, turned into weapons of persecution and mass deportation against specific groups of the population. Learning from these tragic events, the newly formed UN in 1945 made sure not to leave human rights within the sole control of states and subsequently set up an international framework for the protection of human rights to be applied by all states, the beneficiaries being all individuals. "The development of human rights law heralded both a move towards universally recognized rights as well as the possible denationalization of rights."[8]

The Universal Declaration of Human Rights (UDHR) is a milestone document in the development of the international human rights framework. Adopted in 1948, it sets basic standards of achievements for all peoples and all nations in terms of human dignity and rights. Already in its preamble, it affirms "the inherent dignity and the equal and inalienable rights of all members of the human family" as "the foundation of freedom, justice and peace in the world." The UDHR also stresses that "all human beings are born free and equal in dignity and rights" (Article 1) and lays down a number of fundamental human rights to be universally protected. This includes, in Article 15, the right to a nationality, as it states, "(1) Everyone has the right to a nationality. (2) No one shall be arbitrarily deprived of his nationality nor denied the right to change his nationality."

The right to a nationality is therefore a fundamental human right that all human beings on this planet can enjoy, and that all states should ensure for individuals living within their territory. If the right to a nationality is a fundamental human right, then lack of nationality – that is, statelessness – is therefore a human rights violation. Nationality is a gateway to a wide spectrum of basic human rights. Statelessness, or lack of nationality, can thus easily become a catalyst for the violation of the basic rights to which all individuals are entitled, such as the right to education, to own property, to freedom of movement and residence, to social security and health care, to get married, to register the birth of a child, or even to get a death certificate.

Eighteen years after the UDHR was proclaimed, the International Covenant on Civil and Political Rights (ICCPR) and the International Covenant on Economic, Social and Cultural Rights (ICESCR) entered into force in 1966. With these three main international instruments, the International Bill of Human Rights was formed, guaranteeing fundamental human rights applicable to the entire "human family" on the basis that they are human beings – that is, irrespective of their legal status (refugee, migrant, stateless, etc.). Some of these rights include the right to life, to education, to health care, and to freedom of religion or belief, as well as the right to freedom from torture and other degrading and inhuman treatment, from slavery and servitude, and from discrimination based on gender, religion, race, origin, political opinion, etc.

By simply being part of the human family, stateless people are therefore entitled to these fundamental rights as well. And it is the duty of states to avoid new cases of statelessness from emerging. Statelessness therefore occurs when the rights guaranteed by the nationality laws of a given state contradict the fundamental right to a nationality guaranteed by international law.

In practice, gaps do exist between the basic human rights stateless people are entitled to according to international human rights law and the actual state of affairs within each country. Still, we need to be reminded that stateless people are not without rights: they are entitled to many of these fundamental rights provided by international human rights law. By establishing the right to a nationality as a fundamental human right, the International Bill of Human Rights and other international instruments, such as the Statelessness Conventions, include provisions that limit states' capacity to withdraw nationality from their nationals.

The statelessness conventions and other international instruments

A look at the history of the development of international human rights law shows us that as early as the 1920s and 1930s, nationality matters were at the centre of discussions at the League of Nations. The Hague Convention of 1930, held under the auspices of the Assembly of the League of Nations, was the first international attempt to ensure that all persons have a nationality.[9] Indeed, Article 1 of the Hague Convention states, "It is for each State to determine under its own law who are its nationals. This law shall be recognised by other States in so far as it is consistent with international conventions, international custom, and the principles of law generally recognized with regard to nationality." When dealing with nationality matters, states should therefore respect international human rights law provisions, both international treaties and international customary law.

The massive population displacements following WWII brought questions pertaining to nationality, and therefore statelessness, onto the international agenda. The development of international human rights law hence paved the way for the introduction of new international instruments addressing the issue of statelessness.

Other international instruments of human rights law have also been paramount in ensuring that all stateless people are entitled to basic human rights. Two UN instruments specifically dedicated to statelessness form the legal cornerstone in dealing with issues of statelessness: the 1954 Convention relating to the Status of Stateless Persons (1954 Convention) and the 1961 Convention on the Reduction of Statelessness (1961 Convention).

The 1954 Convention is the first international instrument ever adopted providing a definition of stateless people (Article 1), and it also establishes the status of "stateless person" under international law. Originally drafted as a Protocol to the 1951 Convention relating to the Status of Refugees (1951 Refugee Convention), the text became a stand alone Convention in 1954 and is considered "the most comprehensive codification of the rights of stateless persons yet attempted at the international level."[10]

In addition to improving and regulating the status of stateless people, the 1954 Convention guarantees that stateless people access the basic fundamental human rights to which they are entitled. One of its innovations is to provide that identity and travel documents (Articles 27 and 28) are issued for stateless people, who would otherwise face many obstacles in their everyday lives that would render them more vulnerable to marginalization and discrimination. Article 31 prohibits the expulsion of stateless people, except "where compelling reasons of national security otherwise require."

The Convention:

> was adopted to cover, inter alia, those stateless persons who are not refugees and who are not, therefore, covered by the 1951 Convention relating to the Status of Refugees or its Protocol. The 1954 Convention contains provisions regarding stateless persons' rights and obligations pertaining to their legal status in the country of residence. The Convention further addresses a variety of matters which have an important effect on day-to-day life such as gainful employment, public education, public relief, labour legislation and social security. In ensuring that such basic rights and needs are met, the Convention provides the individual with stability and improves the quality of life of the stateless person. This, in turn, can prove to be of advantage to the state in which stateless persons live, since such persons can then contribute to society, enhancing national solidarity and stability. Moreover, the potential for migration or displacement of large population groups decreases, thus contributing to regional stability and peaceful co-existence. [11]

The discussions at the UN Conference on the Elimination or Reduction of Future Statelessness – which met in Geneva in 1959 and in New York City in 1961 – focused mainly on reducing and preventing childhood statelessness, particularly statelessness at birth, as well as on the question of deprivation of nationality. The final text of these deliberations led to the 1961 Convention, which complements the 1954 Convention and provides rules to prevent new cases of statelessness from arising.

The 1961 Convention reminds states that, while the right to determine who is or not a citizen is an element of their sovereignty, states have an obligation to respect international human rights law – that is, to follow internationally contracted agreements and international customary law. The Convention also includes clear and concrete safeguards for avoiding further cases of statelessness from arising. Article 1, for example, provides for the acquisition of nationality for individuals who would otherwise be rendered stateless. States that are parties to the 1961 Convention therefore have an obligation to grant citizenship to children born in their territory, either at birth or upon request, if they would otherwise be stateless, including foundlings (Article 2).

The level of ratification of both the Statelessness Conventions, although on the rise, is still low. In 2014, only 83 states had ratified the 1954 Convention, and 61 states the 1961 Convention.

In addition to the Statelessness Conventions, a number of international legal instruments also provide for the right to a nationality, including the following:

Article 1 of the 1957 Convention on the Nationality of Married Women;

Article 5 (d) (iii) of the 1965 Convention on the Elimination of All Forms of Racial Discrimination;

Article 24 of the 1966 International Covenant on Civil and Political Rights;

Article 9 of the 1979 Convention on the Elimination of All Forms of Discrimination against Women;

Article 7 of the 1989 Convention on the Rights of the Child; and

Article 29 of the 1990 International Convention on the Protection of the Rights of All Migrant Workers and Members of Their Families.

Recently, Article 18 of the 2006 Convention on the Rights of Persons with Disabilities also refers to nationality as a right, recognizing the right of differently abled persons "to liberty of movement, to freedom to choose their residence and to a nationality, on an equal basis with others, including by ensuring that persons with disabilities," as well as "to acquire and change a nationality" and not to be "deprived of their nationality arbitrarily or on the basis of disability."

Regional instruments dealing with nationality

In terms of regional instruments dealing with nationality issues, the 1969 American Convention on Human Rights provides for a right to a nationality in its Article 20:

> 1. Every person has the right to a nationality.
>
> 2. Every person has the right to the nationality of the state in whose territory he was born if he does not have the right to any other nationality.
>
> 3. No one shall be arbitrarily deprived of his nationality or of the right to change it.

The Convention therefore goes further than others in providing safeguards to prevent any cases of childhood statelessness from arising.

The European Convention on Nationality (ECN) is the only regional instrument solely dedicated to the issue of nationality. Adopted by the Council of Europe in 1997, the ECN to date has been ratified by only 20 member states. It confirms the right to a nationality for all and encourages states to ratify the UN Statelessness Conventions.

The ECN encourages the naturalization of long-term residents, and stresses the principle of nondiscrimination on the basis of gender, race, religion, ethnic origin or language. It also deals with the question of multiple nationalities given the current increase in mixed marriages as a result of globalization.

Finally, the 1999 African Charter on the Rights and Welfare of the Child is the most recent regional instrument dealing with nationality issues. Article 6 of the charter provides that

2. Every child shall be registered immediately after birth.

3. Every child has the right to acquire a nationality.

4. States Parties to the present Charter shall undertake to ensure that their Constitutional legislation recognize the principles according to which a child shall acquire the nationality of the state in the territory of which he has been born if, at the time of the child's birth, he is not granted nationality by any other state in accordance with its laws.

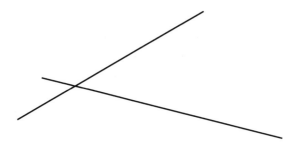

2. Discriminatory Practices

My father came as a refugee to Sweden from Nazi Germany. He had no passport. He was stateless. The Third Reich had stripped him of his nationality. His mother wasn't allowed to join him and was transported away to annihilation in the Nazi camps. In Sweden he wanted to take up his profession. But a Jewish stateless refugee was refused work as a photographer. He went from one unskilled job to the other until retirement as toilet cleaner. His wife, my mother, was a Jewish woman of Russian/Lithuanian origin. I was their only child. In spite of my mother being a Swedish citizen, I was born stateless. As a 4-year-old boy I acquired together with my father Swedish citizenship. In the spirit of "Vergangenheitsbewältigung" Germany remembered my father and in an act of reparation I was given German citizenship.
– Rev. Dr Hans Ucko, interview with author

Discrimination is about treating people and communities unjustly and unfavourably because they are from a particular

ethnic origin or country, or from a particular linguistic affiliation, or because of historical grievances or resentment, or
because they are of a specific gender.

> The growing number of stateless people is neither a
> temporary problem nor the random product of chance
> events. It is the predictable consequence of human rights
> abuses, the result of decisions made by individuals who
> wield power over people's lives. Discrimination and state-
> lessness live side by side; it is no coincidence that most
> stateless people belong to racial, linguistic and religious
> minorities.[1]

This present chapter focuses mainly on discrimination
and lack of equality as an underlying cause of statelessness,
and will particularly explore how discriminatory practices
can affect minorities and women.

Statelessness Resulting from Discrimination against Minorities

Most countries in our current world are multi-ethnic. The
traditional nation-state system, in which a major distinct
national ethnic group corresponded to a delimited territory,
is no longer a reality. The various re-drawings of international
borders in the 20th century and the increasing movement of

people across borders have paved the way for diversity and multi-ethnicity. Today, only very few countries are composed solely of one ethnic or linguistic group.

However, in times of increasing globalization and the apparent tendency toward homogenization, new national narratives are emerging on the importance of maintaining and keeping identities and differences. Such discourse in countries with majority or dominant cultures unfortunately translates into imposing a national identity on minority groups with whom they share a territory – or excluding them from the population. Countries that engage in such discriminatory practices against minority groups sometimes go so far as to denationalize entire communities, rendering them stateless and affecting their basic human rights.

Case studies

Imagine a person who was born and raised in a country, works as a lawyer, is married to a lawyer, and has now started his own family. Life is going well: children are growing, work is prosperous, the couple owns a store and other properties, etc. A new nationality law is enacted, thereby stripping him and his family of their nationality on the pretext that they are descendants of former migrants who came to the country generations ago. This is the story of Dioniso, and many others in the Dominican Republic. In an interview with Open Society Foundations in 2009, he shared his experiences:

I was born here. My wife is a lawyer, originally from Moca. My children . . . are Dominican. I dance merengue. I can't dance Haitian dances. I play baseball. My sons play baseball. I've never been to Haiti. I love everything from the heart of the Dominican Republic, because I am from here.

I went to get my birth certificate. When I arrived, after introducing myself, I say, "I came to get my birth certificate." She doesn't offer me a seat. I explain, "I came here as a citizen to get my birth certificate so that I can go about my life." She says, "Let me see. No I can't give it to you. Because you have a Haitian last name." I say, "How is that possible? Look at my parents' legal status." She says, "I'm not allowed to look at those papers. I have orders not to give birth certificates to anyone with a Haitian last name because we are purifying and cleaning our municipality."

What did I feel? I had to go to the cardiologist. My blood pressure went through the roof for the first time in my life. . . . Your life is just being eliminated . . .
We are Dominicans. We are not enemies . . . I didn't come from Haiti, Jamaica or France. We were born here.[2]

This personal testimony is an illustration of how discrimination can lead to deprivation of nationality, resulting in statelessness. In 2013, a Dominican high court ruling retroactively removed citizenship for Dionisio and an estimated 200,000 Dominicans of Haitian origin, rendering stateless all children born of Haitian immigrant parents who had arrived in the country 50 or 60 years earlier. Most of them are people of Haitian descent, born and raised in the Dominican Republic, sometimes for multiple generations. For decades the Dominican Republic had followed the *jus soli* nationality rule, recognizing the children of Haitian migrants born in the country as Dominican citizens, regardless of the migration status of their parents.

The 2013 court ruling, coupled with other changes in nationality laws designed to address irregular migration from neighbouring Haiti, thus changed overnight the fate of descendants of Haitian migrants. The ruling denies Dominican nationality to be granted to anyone born after 1929 who does not have at least one parent of Dominican blood. In 2014, the government attempted to alleviate and temper the high court ruling with a naturalization law that would recognize the citizenship claims of those affected by the 2013 decision.

Today, Dominicans of Haitian descent are considered as outsiders or illegal migrants in the Dominican Republic. Dioniso's story reveals systematic discrimination against people with French names, who, even after living in the country for various generations, are not considered Dominicans. They cannot, among other things, go to school, get access to health care, open a bank account or ask for a loan, own property, get a driver's license, register the birth of their children, or travel.

Another case of deliberate and intentional isolation of a minority group is the Russian-speaking population of Latvia. Although a Russian minority existed in the territory before Soviet times, more than 265,000 former Soviet citizens who found themselves on Latvian territory were rendered stateless and are now called "non-citizens" because of Latvia's 1994 citizenship law. These are descendants of ethnic Russian Soviet citizens who moved to Latvia during the times of the Soviet Union because they had been left stateless when Latvia gained independence from the Soviet Union and reestablished its 1919 citizenship law. Although they enjoy a wide range of rights, they are not allowed to vote or to stand in public office. They are allowed to become naturalized as Latvian citizens; they first need to pass various tests, including Latvian language and history.

Here is one of the many stories recorded by UNHCR:

Aleksandr is a "non-citizen" born in Riga. He works as a journalist for the Russian service of the national Latvian television and radio. His "non-citizenship saga" began in 1991 when Latvia regained independence. At the time, Aleksandr temporarily lived in Russia, just across the border from Latvia, and could not vote in the referendum for independence. However, his father did vote and did so in support of independence. Aleksandr said that his father had been promised Latvian citizenship but never acquired it, and both have been stateless ever since. Now, Aleksandr lives "with a scar passed on from generation to generation." His 76-year-old father is still "living with a broken promise."[3]

This example reveals how statelessness can result from state succession when it is used as a discriminatory tool to exclude ethnic minorities from the population.

Both case studies illustrate the interconnections between statelessness and discrimination. Deprivation or denial of nationality is used primarily as a weapon to isolate and control a given portion of the population. The affected individuals and their communities consequently face a wide range of vulnerabilities linked to their status as stateless persons. Discrimination can therefore be a cause and a consequence of statelessness.

Nondiscrimination and equality for all

Learning from the atrocities committed during WWII, the international community is well aware of the dangers of intolerance when it comes to minority populations. The UN has advocated for the promotion and protection of minority rights and identities within multi-ethnic states.

Statelessness is an equality issue. When stateless communities exist, it is an indication that the human right to a nationality and the principle of nondiscrimination (Article 2 of UDHR) have not been fulfilled. All human beings, including the stateless, have the fundamental right to be free from discrimination in all aspects of their life. Article 5 (d) (iii) of the 1965 Convention on the Elimination of All Forms of Racial Discrimination also provides for all human beings, "without distinction as to race, colour, or national or ethnic origin, equality before the law" in the enjoyment of a wide array of human rights for all, including the right to nationality.

> While it remains accepted for states to impose certain restrictions on non-citizens concerning the right to vote and to be elected, such restrictions should not be applied more widely than necessary. Denial of citizenship has been used by states to exclude minorities from the enjoyment of their rights. States should consider allowing non-citizens belonging to minorities to vote, stand as candidates in local elections and be members of the governing boards of self-governing bodies, while making sure that access to citizenship is regulated in a non-discriminatory manner.[4]

On 18 December 1992, the UN General Assembly adopted (resolution 47/135) the Declaration on the Rights of Persons Belonging to National or Ethnic, Religious and Linguistic Minorities. It lists a series of rights that minorities are entitled to, such as the right to enjoy their own culture without interference (Article 2.1), and the right to participate effectively in decisions at the national level (Article 2.2).

> Discrimination in any context is an attack on the very notion of universal human rights. It systematically denies certain people their full human rights just because of their colour, race, ethnicity, descent or national origin (or lack of thereof). It is an assault to the fundamental principle underlying the Universal Declaration of Human Rights (UDHR) – that human rights are everyone's birthright and apply to all without distinction.[5]

The principle of nondiscrimination requires states to treat all individuals equally and imposes on states the obligation *to ensure that* all are treated equally by, for instance, identifying and tackling discriminatory practices against any individual, particularly with regard to stateless people. States therefore are obliged to ensure fundamental human rights to all individuals, and to create conducive conditions for all communities within its territory to thrive and prosper.

Statelessness, and the resulting discrimination, is often prolonged by weak governance and lack of rule of law. Good governance plays a major role in including minorities in all aspects of society as well as in guaranteeing them rights and advantages equal to the rest of the population. Media and education can contribute to this process by fostering dialogue, participation, and recognition, which in turn create greater understanding among the various ethnic groups and communities forming the society.

Statelessness has a significant impact on human security, access to development, and enjoyment of human rights.[6] Being stateless means facing various insurmountable obstacles to enjoying basic human rights, such as social exclusion; blocked access to education and health care; physical, moral and sexual violence; and travel restrictions. Stateless people are stigmatized and relegated to a position of secondary importance. They have to struggle on a daily basis to ensure that their basic human rights are respected, facing endless cycles of exclusion and marginalization. This vulnerability is more pronounced for stateless women and children.

Stateless people often live in precarious conditions. Because they lack the identity documents they need to get good jobs, they are often forced to work in the informal sector. When they do manage to get employment, they are offered low wages and can be forced into exploitative jobs in slavery-like conditions. They face difficulties if they attempt to assert their labour rights, which increases their vulnerability to exploitation and prolongs their poverty. Stateless people find themselves trapped in a perpetual cycle of poverty, marginalization, and discrimination that can last for generations.

Depriving specific groups of the population of their nationality can also be a form of government-led discrimination fuelled by politically driven motives. When used as a political weapon of control by states, statelessness can be nurtured by xenophobic and racist policies, which can lead, among other things, to various forms of hate speech. This fuels tensions born out of misjudgments and misinformation. Disenchantment, discontent, and accumulated frustration experienced by stateless communities risk translating into tensions and upheavals, eventually resulting in conflict.

Such cases should be avoided; states should rather promote empowerment through education and ensure adequate housing and access to health care for all. Diversity is a gift. It is a blessing, a richness. It is therefore important to treat everyone with dignity and acknowledge the generations who have lived and contributed to a country.

Signs of hope

A number of countries have taken steps to address cases of statelessness in their country. In the following paragraphs, I present a few examples.

In Ceylon, during the 19th century, the colonial power brought Tamils from India to work on tea and rubber plantations. After Sri Lanka acquired independence in 1947, the Hill Tamils were effectively denied Sri Lankan citizenship. In 2003, UNHCR estimated that around 300,000 Hill Tamils were still stateless in Sri Lanka. But in 2003, the *Grant of Citizenship to Persons of Indian Origin Act* gave immediate citizenship to persons of Indian origin who had resided in Sri Lanka since October 1964, as well as their descendants. This included the Hill Tamils. The act thus essentially ended the problem of statelessness in Sri Lanka. Persons remaining in Sri Lanka of Indian origin went through a simplified process that included signing a declaration of their desire to voluntarily obtain Sri Lankan citizenship.

Another example is Estonia. The situation of stateless ethnic Russians in Estonia is similar to that in Latvia. The issue dates back to Soviet times, during which hundreds of ethnic Russian were forced to move to the Baltic countries, including the present Estonia. When Estonia gained independence, a Citizenship Law adopted in 1992 defined the principles of accession to Estonian nationality through strict application of the *jus sanguinis* principle: that is, by restricting citizenship to those who had links to the country prior to Soviet occupation. Consequently, hundreds of thousands were left stateless. Although many remain stateless today, some have managed to acquire nationality by successfully passing mandatory exams required to obtain citizenship. Moreover, the country is showing new signs of hope: legislation from January 2015 will now allow all children (15 years old and under) who were born stateless in Estonia to acquire nationality. The reform also simplified citizenship requirements for people who are 65 years and older: these are no longer required to pass the written exam of Estonian language that is mandatory for naturalization.

In cases of protracted situations of statelessness, the state may decide to provide legal identity for the concerned individuals. In such cases, these people can either register or declare that they have developed strong ties with the country in which they have been living for many years. Naturalization, although a discretionary decision of the state, is another option to end situations of statelessness. With legal identity, these people will be able to access and enjoy a wide range of the rights that nationals have, such as securing decent work, accessing health care and education, voting and participating in political life, and owning or inheriting property.

This being said, discrimination can sometimes persist due to complex administrative procedures, or to deeply rooted perceptions that must be addressed and healed. In most cases, states are reluctant to naturalize large stateless communities because they are perceived to be a threat to the existing and "fragile" balance in the country's demographic composition.

Just as important as these amendments in nationality laws is the implementation process. Unless governments take necessary and meaningful steps to ensure that stateless communities are well informed about new, positive changes, many will remain ignorant of both the change and the procedures they have to go through to process their naturalization and make their nationality a reality. If there is no implementation, then the reforms risk becoming *lettre morte*. Collaboration between the government and UNHCR, faith communities and civil society, can certainly help in making the reform process a reality, thereby paving the way for new life for stateless communities.

Gender Discrimination in Nationality Laws

Statelessness can also result from discriminatory laws that prevent women from passing on their nationality to their children. Every mother in this world wants what is best for her children. She wants to give them her values, her culture, and all that they need in order to live fulfilling lives, both as children and later as adults. She also wants to pass on to them her nationality, with all the rights attached to it, so that they can belong to the same state.

To date, 27 countries do not treat women and men equally in the laws dealing with attribution of nationality. This is an issue of gender justice, as such laws do not give women and men the same rights in terms of acquiring, retaining, or passing nationality. In Brunei Darussalam, Iran, Kuwait, Lebanon, Qatar, Somalia, and Swaziland mothers are not allowed to confer their nationality on their children in any circumstances. In the Bahamas, Bahrain, Barbados, Burundi, Iraq, Jordan, Liberia, Libya, Madagascar, Malaysia, Mauritania, Nepal, Oman, Saudi Arabia, Sierra Leone, Sudan, Suriname, Syria, Togo, and the United Arab Emirates, although nationality laws do not treat women and men on an equal footing, nationality laws in some instances permit the mother to confer her nationality, for example, where the father is stateless.[7]

From patriarchy to equality

Discrimination against women in nationality laws is inherited from the old principles of "unity of nationality of spouses" and "dependent nationality" that were widely enforced in many countries in the last century. These rules were brought to regions by former colonial powers, and consequently were inherited by new states when they gained their independence.

These principles were strongly rooted in patriarchal considerations, according to which "a woman's legal status is acquired through her relationship to a man – first her father and then her husband" and "that important decisions affecting the family would be made by the husband."[8] When marrying a foreigner, a woman would automatically be given her husband's nationality, and since dual citizenship was little practised then, she would consequently have to renounce her own nationality.

With the development of international human rights law and parallel efforts to put an end to all forms of discrimination, two new instruments relating to women's rights were adopted: the 1957 Convention on the Nationality of

Married Women (1957 Convention) and the 1979 Convention on the Elimination of Discrimination against Women (CEDAW). Both Conventions prohibit any form of overt discrimination against women in citizenship legislations, reaffirming the universal fundamental right to a nationality guaranteed by the UDHR.

Article 1 of the 1957 Convention introduces equality between women and men in terms of nationality, and stresses that "neither the celebration nor the dissolution of a marriage between one of its nationals and an alien, nor the change of nationality by the husband during marriage, shall automatically affect the nationality of the wife." In line with the 1961 Convention (Article 5), Article 9 of the 1979 Convention includes safeguards also for those who risk becoming stateless as a result of a change in civil status:

> 1. States Parties shall grant women equal rights with men to acquire, change or retain their nationality. They shall ensure in particular that neither marriage to an alien nor change of nationality by the husband during marriage shall automatically change the nationality of the wife, render her stateless or force upon her the nationality of the husband.
>
> 2. States Parties shall grant women equal rights with men with respect to the nationality of their children.

Impact of gendered nationality laws

The rationale behind the "unity of nationality of spouses" and the "dependent nationality" principles was originally to unify the family by giving the father's nationality to all members of the family. But the reality proved quite different in many cases: nationality laws that discriminated on the basis of gender ended up not only affecting women, but also breaking the family unit, thereby affecting children and generations to come. In testimony collected in 2013 by the Women's Refugee Commission, for example, a Jordanian national who is married to a stateless man and who is the mother of five stateless children describes her situation:

> Our children have no future. The government doesn't allow the Jordanian mother to pass on her nationality to her children . . . My son works at night, sometimes he leaves at two in the morning; he gets arrested by the police. He doesn't have any documents. Once at two in the morning I had to go and get him . . . Can you imagine? . . . Honestly, it's not a life . . . There's no public sector service that employs our children . . . And they're not allowed to leave this country . . . they can't leave . . . This is my house. After I die, my children cannot inherit it from me . . . It's a disaster in the real sense of the word . . . My oldest son is 29 years old. Nobody is going to marry my

children, because it will only lead to problems . . . I paid for their education through loans that I'm still paying off.[9]

This testimony is not an isolated case. In countries where women do not enjoy equal rights with men in terms of nationality laws, such laws become "a collective sentence: a woman's inability to pass her nationality to her children punishes everyone related to the woman."[10]

Nationality laws that discriminate according to gender also lead to stateless children in cases where they are unable to acquire their father's nationality. This can be for a number of reasons: for example, when the father is stateless; is absent or unknown; is unwilling or unable due to complex or expensive administrative steps; or because it is against the nationality laws of his country (for instance, in cases when a child is born outside of wedlock).

The impact on the livelihood of the children and the larger family has such repercussions that it can become an inter-generational issue. For instance, in countries where mothers cannot confer nationality to their children, women may be reluctant to marry a stateless man because their children will automatically become stateless as well.

Furthermore, children who are born stateless have difficulties accessing public education, which will have a huge impact on their future chances of finding employment in their adulthood. With no education, low-paying jobs, and many other obstacles to their enjoying even basic social rights, they are unable to provide financial stability for their families, thus exacerbating their precarious living conditions and poverty.

Statelessness resulting from such discrimination also has detrimental effects on the emotional wellbeing of the mother and her descendants. Mothers feel guilt, shame, or hopelessness over not being able to help their stateless children and for letting down their families. The children, facing constant rejection and obstacles in their attempts to lead a fulfilling and prosperous life, feel frustrated, depressed, and worthless.

Stateless by marriage

The principles of "unity of nationality of spouses" and "dependent nationality" had other far-reaching consequences in the lives of women and their family members. For instance, a woman who marries a foreigner but who continues to reside in her own country may be deprived of her nationality of origin, and will become a foreigner in the country she always called home, thereby losing all the rights she was entitled to as a national. She will become totally dependent on her husband.

Also according to this principle, if the foreign husband loses or changes his nationality, the changes may automatically be applied to the wife. If their marriage ends, either through divorce or death of the husband, the wife will retain her husband's nationality only if the legislation provides so. If not, she must attempt to regain her original nationality. Otherwise, she will become stateless.

These situations are a reality for many women today, particularly in the case of "economic brides." These are women who enter into arranged marriages with a foreign husband in the hopes of escaping poverty or precarious living conditions. If these marriages break down, these women find themselves without any nationality, because they had to renounce their own nationality to take their husband's. The cases reported by UNHCR include Vietnamese women marrying Taiwanese husbands, or Uzbek women who marry citizens of Kyrgyzstan. As one reports states, "Thousands of Vietnamese women who married Taiwanese men were left stateless because they were forced to renounce their citizenship in order to apply for citizenship in Taiwan. But if their marriages broke up before they got their new nationality, they – and often their children – came back to Vietnam stateless, even in the country of their birth."[11]

One example is the story of Loan, a woman originally from Vietnam. Her parents advised her to marry a Taiwanese man who promised to "whisk her out of poverty," and so she renounced her Vietnamese nationality. She became pregnant with their second child as she started processing her Taiwanese citizenship, and returned to Vietnam to have a baby girl. When the second child also turned out to be a girl, the husband "left and disappeared for ever." She now lives with her grandmother and her two children, "deserted by a husband who won't even take her phone calls."[12] Loan is stateless today, because she had to renounce her nationality and has not acquired Taiwanese citizenship. She could not get legal employment and so works in the informal economy. She has not been able to register her children, who are thus not eligible for the social services provided to Vietnamese citizens. Her children are not entitled to the free education reserved for nationals, so she is accumulating debt in order to pay for private schools.

These hundreds of thousands of "economic brides" in various parts of the world see their hopes and dreams of a good life deteriorate and collapse. In addition to the risks of becoming stateless, some tell tales of alcoholic, abusive husbands, cruel mothers-in-law, cramped living quarters, deprivation, and economic exploitation. They also suffer from language barriers that hamper any new relationships improving over time. Their plight should be an incentive for governments to ratify both of the Statelessness Conventions as well as the CEDAW, and to take all necessary steps to guarantee that women and men are equal before the law in the retention, acquisition, and transmission of nationality.

Signs of hope

In our current globalized world, the number of mixed marriages is increasing, leading to new cases of conflict in nationality laws. This can result in statelessness, particularly in situations where a divorced woman cannot pass her nationality to her children or regain her previous nationality. However, over the last 13 years, nearly 15 countries have changed their nationality laws and are now granting equal rights to men and women in relation to acquisition, retention, or transmission of nationality. These countries include Sri Lanka, Egypt, Algeria, Indonesia, Bangladesh, Zimbabwe, Kenya, Tunisia, and Senegal. These positive reforms have greatly contributed to improving the lives of individuals and their families, who would otherwise be stateless.

Nondiscrimination between women and men in the conferral of nationality to children can be achieved by ensuring gender-neutral nationality legislations allowing all nationals, irrespective of gender, to pass on their nationality to their children. The following subsections provide some examples of countries that illustrate what can be achieved when the political will is present.

EGYPT

In 2004, Egypt reformed its nationality laws and now allows both parents to equally pass on their Egyptian nationality to their children. This means that a child is considered Egyptian if at least one of his parents is Egyptian. This reform has greatly improved the lives of many families who were struggling with on-going discrimination and living in fear of deportation. The amendment originally excluded stateless children of a Palestinian father, "the argument being that this would 'protect' their right of return to Palestine." But thanks to efforts by civil society and affected families, the amendment now applies to them as well. The amendments, however, do not allow Egyptian women to pass on their nationality to their spouse, as Egyptian men can. In other words, a foreign man married to an Egyptian woman cannot acquire Egyptian nationality; however, the reverse is possible when an Egyptian man marries a foreign woman.

INDONESIA

The 1958 citizenship law No. 62 in Indonesia exclusively granted nationality through the father's line. If a foreign man married an Indonesian woman, their children would automatically become foreigners, despite their having an Indonesian mother or being born and raised in the country. Being considered foreigners, they had to leave Indonesia every year to renew their residence permit. This changed in 2006, when "Indonesia adopted a new Citizenship Law which, at least with regard to gender equality, is a model for other countries."[13] Recognizing that the right to a nationality is a fundamental human right all individuals should enjoy irrespective of gender, the new law introduced a gender-neutral definition of citizenship that gives equal rights to women and men to pass on their nationality to their children, whether married or not.

ALGERIA

Prior to the new nationality reforms introduced in 2005, the Algerian Nationality Code allowed Algerian mothers to pass their Algerian nationality to their children only if the father was stateless, unknown, or a foreigner born in Algeria. In cases of children born in Algeria from a foreign father born abroad and residing in the country, these children were allowed to apply for Algerian nationality once they reached the age of 18. As a UNHCR report states:

> The new Nationality Code repeals the limitations on Algerian mothers' ability to confer nationality on their children, replacing them with a simple overarching provision granting Algerian nationality to all children born in or outside Algeria to an Algerian mother or father without distinction. These revised provisions of the code apply with retroactive effect. As a result, individuals born to Algerian mothers and foreign fathers before the reform are also considered nationals; thus the reform not only serves to prevent future statelessness but also to resolve existing cases.[14]

As all of these cases show, discrimination against women in nationality laws has far-reaching consequences for the members of the family, and particularly the children. This is an area where gender-based discrimination in the attribution of nationality intersects with childhood statelessness.

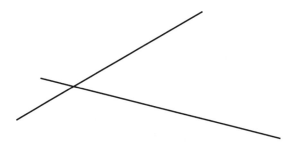

3. Stateless Children

The birth of a child is an important event in the life of a family. Children are a gift: they bring joy to their parents' lives and to the family at large. They are an extension of their family: they ensure continuity and lineage. They are filled with innocence when they come into this world.

According to the UNHCR, a stateless baby is born at least every ten minutes.[1] They inherit their parents' lack of legal status and are swept into inextricable situations for which they are not responsible and over which they have no control. They are born into lives that will be filled with hurdles, complications, rejections, and discrimination. They grow up being reminded every day that they are not entitled to many basic rights because they are "different," because they do not belong to any country. They will grow up witnessing the daily struggles of their parents and members of their community, exposed to discrimination and precarious life styles. Stateless children do not receive many opportunities to live as carefree children: they have responsibilities, worries, and challenges thrust upon them at an early age.

Causes of Childhood Statelessness

Children can become stateless or can risk becoming stateless in several ways. They can inherit the lack of legal status from their parents. This is the case, for instance, when the criteria for attribution of nationality articulated by the state are based on exclusive and discriminatory lines. In other words, ethnic, linguistic, or religious minorities within a population, including their descendants, are made stateless through the operation of the laws of the state. We saw this in the aforementioned case of stateless communities in the Dominican Republic, where children born of stateless parents of Haitian descent will also automatically become stateless: they will experience the same rejection and discrimination as their parents. The same applies to children born in communities that have been purposely left out by a state during state succession. An illustration would be children from the Russian-speaking population in Latvia. Because their parents are considered "non-residents," they will inherit the same lack of legal status and also become stateless.

In countries where men and women are not treated equally in terms of attribution of nationality, children born to a single mother or to a foreign father who cannot pass his nationality will automatically become stateless. The same applies to children whose father is stateless, absent, or unknown. As Amal, a Lebanese national and mother of nine-year-old Rama, who is stateless, told UNHCR:

> My children don't have nationality because their grandfather was stateless and their father is stateless too and I can't do anything for my children. In the Lebanese system, the mother cannot transmit nationality to her children or husband . . . If my children's situation doesn't change, they have no future.[2]

In such countries, which practise gender inequality in nationality laws, only men are allowed to pass on their nationality to the children. Mothers thus feel powerless, involuntarily condemning their children to a life as outsiders, as stateless persons within their own country. It is a difficult burden to carry as a parent, and particularly as a mother, when all they aspire for is to provide their children with the best options in life. Children become a kind of "collateral damage" in a discriminatory system they did not create but have to endure.

Children can also become stateless when they fall through gaps in nationality laws between countries: in other words, when they do not meet the criteria to obtain nationality in any country. For instance, if a child is born out of wedlock in Switzerland to a British mother, who was born to a Dutch mother and raised in the Netherlands, and a Danish father, who was living and working in Switzerland for a few years, the child will be stateless for the following reasons:

> The child is not able to receive Danish nationality because the couple is unmarried and the child has been born outside of Denmark.
>
> The mother cannot pass her British nationality to her child because she was born in the Netherlands of a Dutch mother; British nationality law prevents second generations born outside Great Britain to acquire British nationality.
>
> The child cannot be Swiss because Switzerland does not follow the *jus soli* rule in terms of acquisition of nationality.

For the child to acquire Dutch nationality, the mother first has to be naturalized Dutch. However, the mother is not living in the Netherlands anymore, and she needs to live there at least five years in order to be able to apply for Dutch citizenship. In the meantime, the newborn will be stateless.

With the increase of mixed marriages as a result of globalization and international migration, the number of children who are stateless because they are caught between the cracks of nationality laws of various countries will continue to increase unless states include safeguards in their nationality laws to prevent children from becoming stateless at birth. Childhood statelessness is preventable: all it takes is the political commitment and will of states to frame their legislation so that no child will be born stateless on their territory.

Abandoned children, that is, foundlings, are also very vulnerable to becoming stateless if there is no information about who their parents are or where they were born. This is the case for children abandoned, for instance, in front of churches and hospitals. Since they do not appear in any official records, children whose origin is unknown can be treated as stateless persons in countries where nationality is acquired solely on descent (*jus sanguinis*). Adoption or naturalization can help these children acquire a nationality and solve their statelessness. Fortunately, in countries that have ratified the 1961 Convention, these foundlings are automatically granted citizenship because they are "considered to have been born within that territory of parents possessing the nationality of that state" (Article 2, 1961 Convention). In other words, these foundlings will be considered citizens of the country in which they were found.

The Impact of Statelessness on Children

For children, being stateless means that they will inherit and experience the same patterns of exclusion and discrimination as their parents. From an early age, they find themselves in situations where they are not treated equal to their peers simply because they are not legally recognized and do not, for example, possess an identity card where one is required. This surely leaves them with psychological scars, instilling in them a sense of worthlessness, disillusion, and injustice – a sense of being "different."

In many countries, stateless children are excluded from public education. In some states, they are allowed to enrol in schools, but are asked to show an identity document when they need to write national exams. Because stateless children have no travel documents, they cannot benefit from scholarship programmes abroad, or even class trips. Parents of stateless children often go out of their way to provide opportunities for their children, sending them to private school and thus acquiring huge debts to secure a decent education. Even when parents manage to enroll their stateless children in private schools for primary and secondary education, fees for higher education are often excessive. As a result, the child's chances of securing a stable and well-paid job in the future remain limited.[3]

Even when they manage to get diplomas or school certificates, stateless children risk being barred from government jobs and other employment opportunities as adults. Their lack of identity documents and legal status are real obstacles in securing jobs that meet their potential, ambitions, and needs, and they often resort to vocational training in order to be able to secure a job quickly. A UNHCR report describes the experiences of a stateless mother in Malaysia:

> Kavita in Malaysia wanted to teach art but no college would admit her because she was stateless. Undeterred, she applied for a job with the local nursery school, but despite excelling during the interview she was refused employment because she could not set up a bank or pension account. Now, she works in a friend's grocery store. "It's a dead-end job," says Kavita. "But, for now this job has been very helpful since I don't have proof of any nationality and can't work anywhere else. But I wish to become a teacher. It's been my ambition since I was very young. I now tutor children at my uncle's house. It's how I keep my dream alive.[4]

For those coming from poor families, securing a well-paid job is the new dawn of a better life for the entire family, a chance to leave behind a precarious and challenging life.

In many countries, stateless people and their children do not have access to public health care, including governmental health campaigns for vaccination, for HIV/AIDS prevention, or emergency medical assistance in case of accidents. In many countries, health facilities ask for an identity document in order to provide treatment. Also, many stateless mothers give birth at home, thus increasing risk of mortality for both the mother and the child. Neither of them has access to adequate and timely natal care. In addition, a child born at home is rarely registered, which leaves the child without any trace in official records.

In times of emergencies, both armed conflicts and natural disasters, children are usually vulnerable to being displaced, exploited, recruited as child soldiers, detained, or being separated from their families. Stateless children are particularly vulnerable in such circumstances. Without any documents proving who they are and where they belong, they can spend years being unable to trace their families. They also risk being detained indefinitely without appearing in any records.

Growing up in precarious and poor economic conditions, stateless children can also end up as street children. As part of the need to survive in a tough environment, they find themselves involved in gangs and petty offences, as a result facing trouble with the judicial system. Also, because they are unable to prove their age, they can be mistaken for adults and consequently incarcerated with and tried as adults.

Stateless children are particularly vulnerable to exploitation. Their lack of legal identity leaves them vulnerable to abuse, exploitation, and trafficking. Since there is no precise information about their age, stateless children are not protected against child labour and other forms of exploitation. The UNHCR cites examples of cases:

> Mistreatment can take different forms as stateless children grow older. Clémentine (22) and Odile (21) are stateless sisters living in Abidjan, Côte d'Ivoire. When they were very young they were made to work in a restaurant and later forced into prostitution by the aunt in whose care they had been placed as small children. Lacking the protection of nationality documents they found themselves trapped. Only after the situation became intolerable did they find the courage to flee.[5]

Having no identity documents, stateless children also become easy prey for unscrupulous traffickers who can easily smuggle them to other countries and threaten to report them to authorities if they do not comply with their rules. In particular, traffickers can force stateless girls into prostitution and sexual bondage, or sell them as "brides." They can also push them into servitude, forcing them to work as domestics in slave-like conditions, or making them work in hazardous conditions that can put their lives at risk.

Lack of identity therefore translates into a life of abuse, exploitation, disillusionment, and disenfranchisement for millions of stateless children. The development of international human rights law heralded protection and rights to all children, and *a fortiori* to stateless children.

Children's Right to a Nationality

Children's human rights law was developed to preserve children from human rights violations, to preserve their innocence, and make sure that all decisions taken in their names are made in their best interest. As I explained in Chapter 1 of this book, Article 15 of the UDHR establishes the right to a nationality for all individuals. Children are therefore also equally entitled to the fundamental human right to a nationality.

The 1961 Convention on the Reduction of Statelessness contains several articles about the acquisition of nationality by children. Article 1 grants nationality to "a person born in its territory who would otherwise be stateless," either by application of the law or upon application. This is a key provision to prevent new cases of childhood statelessness from arising, because it obliges the signatory state to give nationality to a child who would otherwise become stateless. As the UNCHR's guidelines on statelessness referring to the 1961 convention state:

The 1961 Convention further includes provisions for acquisition of the mother's nationality by descent if the child was born in the mother's state and would otherwise be stateless (Article 1.3), acquisition of the nationality of a parent by descent via an application procedure for individuals who do not acquire nationality of the state of birth (Article 1.4), and on acquisition of the nationality of a parent by descent for individuals born abroad who would otherwise be stateless (Article 4). Article 2 contains a provision regulating nationality of foundlings while Article 3 establishes a rule regulating the territorial scope of the Convention.[6]

The 1989 Convention on the Rights of the Child (CRC) is to date the main international instrument dealing with child's rights. It is the most widely ratified international treaty – with 194 ratifying states out of 196 – and it is therefore the most authoritative international convention for protecting children's human rights. The CRC upholds various principles applicable to children, such as their fundamental human right to nondiscrimination; the need to secure the best interests of the child; the right to life, survival, and development of children; and their right to participate. These principles are essential to ensure children's dignity, protection, and wellbeing. In line with the UDHR, Article 7 of the CRC upholds children's "right from birth to a name, the right to acquire a nationality" and adds that "States Parties shall ensure the implementation of these rights in accordance with their national law and their obligations under the relevant international instruments in this field, in particular where the child would otherwise be stateless."

Unfortunately, ratification of international instruments and implementation do not always go hand in hand. Given the nearly universal ratification the CRC received from states, one would expect that children's rights would be at its apogee. The reality is quite saddening: millions in the world today are stateless. The right to a nationality enshrined in Article 7 of the CRC is *lettre morte* in these countries. Such inaction by states has a profound impact on the lives, hopes, and future of these stateless children.

States should therefore give primary consideration to the welfare and wellbeing of children in any decisions concerning children. The principle of the best interest of the child (Article 3 of the CRC) should be at the core of any decisions involving children. With regard to the right to a nationality, this principle requires children to be protected from becoming stateless. In other words, the best interest of stateless children is to acquire a nationality.

Children's right to a nationality is also affirmed in various international instruments. For instance, Article 24 of the ICCPR states that "every child shall be registered immediately after birth and shall have a name" and that "every child has the right to acquire a nationality." This is also asserted in Article 29 of the 1990 International Convention on the Protection of the Rights of All Migrant Workers and Members of Their Families (Convention on Migrant Workers), which provides that "each child of a migrant worker shall have the right to a name, to registration of birth and to a nationality." More recently, Article 18 of the 2006 Convention on the Rights of Persons with Disabilities recognizes that children "shall be registered immediately after birth and shall have the right from birth to a name, the right to acquire a nationality and, as far as possible, the right to know and be cared for by their parents."

In all decisions involving children, the primary concern should therefore be the wellbeing, development, and fulfilment of children. It is about making the decisions that will allow them to enjoy their childhood, meet their essential needs, and help them grow and achieve their potential as much as possible.

Birth Registration: A Protection and Prevention Tool

Birth registration is another fundamental right to which all children, irrespective of their legal status, are entitled. Churches and most religious institutions have for centuries been registering and keeping track of important life events such as birth, baptism, marriage, and death. The same is done in our modern secular world.

Proof of legal existence

Birth registration is the first official record attesting that a child is born – that the child exists. It indicates who the parents of the child are, as well as where and when the child was born. These are key details in establishing the nationality of the child. This document records under the law the relationships between the newborn and his or her family members, the link between the child and the nationality of his or her parents, and the connection between the newborn and the country of birth.

According to the Office of the High Commissioner for Human Rights,

> Birth registration is the continuous, permanent and universal recording within the civil registry of the occurrence and characteristics of birth, in accordance with the national legal requirements. It establishes the existence of a person under law, and lays the foundation for safeguarding civil, political, economic, social and cultural rights. As such, it is a fundamental means of protecting the human rights of the individual.[7]

The child's right to have his or her birth registered is a fundamental human right: Article 7 of the 1989 Convention on the Rights of the Child (CRC) stipulates, "The child shall be registered immediately after birth." It also reaffirms children's right to a legally registered name and to be officially recognized by the state in which they are born. It further recognizes children's right to a nationality and thereby to belong to a country.

Birth registration is thus just one of various civil registration systems, including marriage, death, divorce, and adoption. Even apart from establishing a person's legal identity, these records provide statistics that give the government concrete indications of the demographics in the country. The data collected are in turn useful to the state to plan socio-economic policies which will benefit the different groups of the population. However, birth registration also has the fundamental function of proving one's existence, and it is a right to which all children, irrespective of their legal status, are entitled.

Birth registration, however, does not provide a nationality to the child. It is only a document proving legal existence. This being said, it contains all the information necessary to establish the child's nationality and is a proof of the child's existence under the law. In other words, the information contained reflects our nationality, our link to a state. Children born to non-nationals should therefore also be registered in the country where they are born. For instance, a child born in Switzerland of Ethiopian parents will be registered in the Swiss civil registry as an Ethiopian child born to Ethiopian parents in Switzerland. The child is Ethiopian, not Swiss, because both Switzerland and Ethiopia apply the *jus sanguinis* rule in attributing nationality. In other words, for a child to be a Swiss national at birth, at least one parent has to be Swiss. A contrasting example would be a child born in Canada to a French mother and an Italian father. Because Canada applies the *jus soli* rule, the child would acquire the nationality both of the parents and of the country. Since all three countries allow dual or multiple nationalities, the child will therefore be able to acquire all three nationalities: Canadian, French, and Italian.

Although mixed marriage can entitle children to dual – or more – nationalities, some children are less fortunate and become victims of gaps in citizenship laws. Consequently, they become stateless, as we saw in the aforementioned case of the child born out of wedlock in Geneva to a British mother (born in the Netherlands to a Dutch mother) and a Danish father. Birth registration is therefore a very important official record in helping to establish the legal identity of children, their very existence in the eyes of the law. It is also an essential official record in determining whether newborns can acquire citizenship on the basis of parentage (*jus sanguinis*) or place of birth (*jus soli*).

By proving the legal existence of a child and providing information about his or her nationality, birth registration is an essential tool in preventing statelessness. Once it is determined that a child is stateless, the parents can start legal procedures to make sure their child can acquire at least one of their nationalities, or the nationality of the country the child was born in. If the child is born of stateless parents in a country that has ratified the 1961 Convention, then the child can acquire the nationality of the place of birth: Article 1 stipulates that "a contracting state shall grant its nationality to a person born in its territory who would otherwise be stateless."

Birth registration also enables the child to get a birth certificate. "A birth certificate is a certified extract from the birth registration; as such it is a document that proves the registration."[8] It is thus a document produced based on information found in the birth registration.

Millions of unregistered births

Despite the pivotal role of registering a child's birth, more than 229 million births go unregistered every year according to United Nations Children's Fund (UNICEF) statistics.[9] The rates of birth registration vary among regions: Europe, Latin America, and the Caribbean have the highest rates in terms of birth registration, and the lowest rates are found in Africa and Asia. According to a UNICEF report,

> Globally, South Asia has the largest number of unregistered children, with approximately 22.5 million, or over 40 per cent of the world's unregistered births in 2000. In

sub-Saharan Africa, 70 per cent of all births went unregistered in 2000. In South Asia, the figure was 63 per cent. In the Middle East and North Africa, nearly one third of the children born in 2000 were unregistered, while in East Asia and the Pacific, 22 per cent of births were not registered.[10]

Children may lack birth registration for any number of reasons, for example, due to complex and onerous administrative procedures, the remoteness of the birthplace, the distance to the closest civil registry office, or simply the parents' ignorance of the importance of registering the birth. Cultural reasons could also arise, for instance in situations where a child is traditionally named several days after the birth. Some people may also avoid registering their newborn out of fear: for instance, single mothers in countries where having a child out of wedlock is not well perceived, or parents with an irregular status who want to remain unnoticed by the state. Gender discrimination can also be a cause for the lack of birth registration: in some countries, women are not allowed to register the birth of their child. Such discrimination particularly affects single mothers.

In any event, birth registration should be done systematically for all newborns. It should be made accessible to all, irrespective of the parents' nationality or residence status. Ideally, it should be free, but if not, then it should demand minimal costs. A recent success story in this vein is the case of Tanzania. In the fall of 2015, the country launched a national campaign allowing parents to register the birth of a child through mobile phone. "The new system being rolled out across the country over the next five years allows a health worker to send the baby's name, sex, date of birth and family details by phone to a central data base and a birth certificate is issued free of charge in days."[11] It is to be hoped that such a campaign will be replicated in countries experiencing low birth registration rates, as the lack of birth registration can pose serious challenges to children which, as we will see below, they will continue to experience even as adults.

Risks ensuing from lack of birth registration

Birth registration is a human right. It is a fundamental right to be protected by the law. It is the primary form of documenting one's existence under the law. All children are entitled to have their birth registered, irrespective of whether their parents are non-nationals, refugees, irregular migrants, or stateless people. The Office of the High Commissioner for Human Rights reports,

> While birth registration does not in itself confer citizenship on a child, it is essential to ensure the right of every child to acquire a nationality, as it constitutes an important form of proof of the link between an individual and

the state. It documents where a child was born and who the child's parents are, thus providing important evidence of whether a child can acquire citizenship on the basis of place of birth (*jus soli*) or of descent (*jus sanguinis*).[12]

Children whose birth is not registered start life with a serious disadvantage. This is even more the case if their lack of birth registration results in statelessness. A birth certificate, or registration, is necessary to receive identity documents, which in turn will be required to establish nationality or to get other essential documents, such as a driver's license or a social security card. Many countries require people to have a birth certificate or any form of civil registry in order to access the public health-care system (including national health campaigns), to open a bank account, or to enroll in the education system. In our modern world, we need to have identification to access a wide range of basic services, or simply, for example, to purchase a mobile phone and get a sim card. Without an identity document, we would have no access to many of the things we enjoy and take for granted.

Lack of birth registration is therefore a major obstacle for unregistered children, and particularly for those who are also stateless, i.e., completely invisible to the system. Without any documents witnessing their legal existence, their name, or their age, non-registered and stateless children are completely invisible to the system. This makes them even more vulnerable to exploitation, discrimination, and abuse. Non-registered and stateless children from marginalized communities will thus continue to experience violations of human rights, just as their stateless parents did.

Girls who have no documents to prove their age can become victims of child or forced marriage. According to UNICEF:

> Worldwide, more than 700 million women alive today were married as children. More than 1 in 3 – or some 250 million – were married before 15. Girls who marry before they turn 18 are less likely to remain in school and more likely to experience domestic violence. Young teen-age girls are more likely to die due to complications in pregnancy and childbirth than women in their 20s; their infants are more likely to be stillborn or die in the first month of life.[13]

Child marriage is thus a form of violence against women: it deprives girls of their innocence and strips them of their childhood. It is an abomination that can be prevented by changing harmful traditional practices and mentalities, but also by documenting the age of all children. Information about their age will allow them to bring their cases to court, particularly when they have experienced domestic violence and other forms of abuse.

Children whose age is unknown due to lack of registration can also become victims of child labour and end up working long hours in hazardous conditions. Even with state legislation prohibiting child labour, children risk not being protected if they cannot prove their age. Unscrupulous employers will be tempted to exploit such vulnerable children and hire them at very low wages. Furthermore, without any information regarding their ages, non-registered stateless children in conflict with the law risk being mistaken for and tried as adults for offences they committed as minors. They will be detained with adults, and face same sentences, including the death penalty in some countries.

Birth registration is also essential to protect children from exploitative practices such as trafficking. Non-registered and stateless children are more vulnerable by child traffickers because of the lack of any document to trace their existence. Children falling into the hands of such criminals can easily be commodified and sold, abroad or locally, into forced labour, including as child soldiers, or sexual servitude. Since they appear nowhere in the official records, their plight will remain unknown, hidden. "Law enforcement agencies cannot prosecute traffickers without proof of the age and identity of those trafficked."[14]

During armed conflict situations and the resulting population displacements, both within the state or to neighbouring countries, lack of identification documents becomes a hindrance to family reunification. Non-registered stateless children are difficult to trace because their identity is not established anywhere. With the current refugee crisis resulting from political turmoil and conflict in the Middle East, the hundreds of thousands of unregistered births of Syrian refugee children are threatening to create a generation of stateless children. As explained previously, Syrian nationality law discriminates against women in terms of attribution of nationality, as well as birth registration.

With families ripped apart as a result of the conflict and the ensuing uprootedness, children born without the presence of their fathers – who are dead, fighting, or missing – are at great risk of becoming stateless. If they want to return to their homeland once the war is over, children who were born in exile without fathers will have a difficult time asserting their Syrian citizenship. As Refugees International reports, "Depending on how the civil war ends and what will be included in the process of reconciliation, hundreds of thousands of Syrian babies and children could be made stateless, not because they don't have a rightful claim to nationality, but because they can't prove that claim."[15] The best way to prevent the risk of statelessness for these children is to amend Syrian nationality law so that mothers can, on an equal basis as men, register the birth of their children and confer their Syrian citizenship on them.

It is important to stress again that while birth registration prevents statelessness, it does not automatically mean that the state registering the birth grants nationality to the child. For instance, a Syrian child born and registered in Switzerland, Lebanon, or Malaysia will not acquire any of these nationalities; the registration document is instead evidence that the child is entitled to claim his or her parents' Syrian citizenship by *jus sanguinis*.

Chaplains and other religious leaders may also be able to document the birth of these children born on migratory routes or in makeshift refugee camps. Baptismal records or other birth records from religious groups have been used for centuries as evidence to prove people's existence. Such documents can provide the necessary information to help establish the birth certificates for these children when the war is over.

In contexts of emergencies, of either natural disasters or armed conflicts, birth records are sometimes destroyed. Some people may lose their documents when they are fleeing the war; others lose them when their homes or the civil registry office are destroyed. In these circumstances, it will be difficult to legally document and confirm not just a child's nationality, but its mere existence. It is thus important for governments to digitally record births in order to secure sensitive information pertaining to the nationals and non-nationals living in their territory.

Birth registration is therefore about protection, security, and safety. It is important that states do not minimize the importance and value of proper birth registration systems in their country, not only as a good governance tool to develop custom-made child-friendly policies, but also as an essential element of establishing the legal existence of newborns, irrespective of their parents' nationality or residence status. Birth registration is a safeguard – a protection tool for children and their future life as adults.

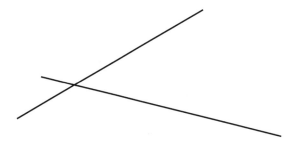

4. Statelessness and Displacement

The UNHCR estimates that there are at least 10 million stateless persons in the world today. This figure however does not include stateless persons who are also refugees, that is, those who have left their country and sought refuge abroad. The reason is mainly to avoid counting the same individuals twice. In other words, stateless refugees are counted as "refugees," while those who have not sought refuge in another country are listed as "stateless persons." According to the UNHCR, there are today close to two million refugees who are also stateless.

Living as a refugee or as an asylum seeker in a foreign country with no documentation papers is quite a challenge. Being stateless is an additional hardship added to the many challenges such people have to juggle. Stateless refugees experience innumerable obstacles and hardships arising from being outside their country of origin. They often lead precarious lives filled with uncertainty, marginalization, and discrimination. They face poverty and may have experienced trauma from witnessing and surviving armed conflict. They have lost family ties and households, and they must adjust to a new cultural, social, and linguistic environment. Women and girls who are stateless refugees are disproportionately vulnerable during all stages of displacement, and can easily become victims of sexual and gender-based violence.

Issues of statelessness and uprootedness can therefore be intermingled, and also influence one another. Statelessness can be a cause for displacement (A), and in some instances it can become a consequence of displacement (B). As a result of their lack of documentation, stateless persons in displacement contexts also become more vulnerable and exposed to being detained or exploited by traffickers (C).

Statelessness: A Cause of Displacement

Lacking the normal rights of citizens, refugees are subject to the caprice of the host nation. Paradoxically, the very ideas of nationality and citizenship deprive human beings of their rights the moment they leave their own polity. The resulting "natural" response of states has been to contain the stateless within refugee camps, isolating them from the normal civic and social life of the host nation.
– Ben Reynolds, "The State against the Stateless,"
The Diplomat (20 November 2014)

The condition of being stateless can be a strong push factor for individuals facing persecution as a result of their lack of legal status. Migrating abroad or fleeing persecution sometimes seems the only plausible solution for these individuals and their families. In their search for a better future, stateless people lose their sense of belonging or of being "rooted" when forced to leave their country of birth, the place they used to call home – even though they were never considered as belonging to that place.

One illustration of how statelessness can be a cause for displacement is the case of the Rohingya, a people who fled from their country of birth, Myanmar. The Rohingya are an ethnic Muslim minority that has lived in the Rakhine state in Myanmar for generations. Approximately more than a million of Rohingya are estimated to live in Myanmar today, and hundreds of thousands of them have fled to and sought refuge in neighbouring Bangladesh and Thailand, as well as other Southeast Asian and Gulf countries. The government of Myanmar does not recognize them as citizens despite their strong ties with the country, and they are known today to be the largest stateless group in the world and one of the most persecuted minority groups.

In December 2011, the Commission of the Churches on International Affairs (CCIA) organized four simultaneous solidarity visits to Bangladesh and Nepal to visit stateless refugee communities in both countries. In Bangladesh, one of the delegations visited Kutupalong and Nayapara, two government-run refugee camps near the Cox's Bazar area hosting nearly 30,000 Rohingya from the Rakhine state in Myanmar. Basic water, sanitation, and health services are provided by the government, UNHCR, and its partners.[1]

Outside the registered camps, the delegation had the opportunity to visit the makeshift camps where more than 250,000 unregistered Rohingya lived in slum-like conditions. These Rohingya people have been living in these camps for many years, some for decades.

Rohingya have been denied citizenship as a result of a disputed interpretation of history. The government of Myanmar considers that the Rohingya arrived in the country at the time of British colonization in the late nineteenth century and are therefore "illegal immigrants" from neighbouring Bangladesh:

> In reality, the Rohingya have had a well-established presence in what is now (Myanmar) since at least the twelfth century. . . . A second wave of migration took place in the fifteenth century, and Rohingya give as further evidence of their long settlement in Arakan the fact that the kings of Arakan from 1400 to 1600 took Muslim (as well as Buddhist) names. In 1784, the Burman King Bodawpaya conquered and incorporated the Arakan region into his kingdom of Ava in central Burma. . . . The British

colonized Burma in a series of three wars beginning in 1824. This period witnessed significant migration of laborers to Burma from neighboring South Asia. The British administered Burma as a province of India, thus migration to Burma was considered an internal movement.[2]

In 1982, the government of Myanmar set up a nationality law by which 135 ethnic groups acquired the Myanmarese nationality because they belong, according to the government, to original "national races," that is, to those that were present in the territory before 1823, the time British settlers arrived. By not recognizing the Rohingya as citizens, the 1982 law overtly excluded them from the population, thus denying them any possibility to become full citizens and to contribute to the country as the other ethnic groups. They have since been living in limbo and also have become the targets of hate campaigns depriving them of basic rights and policies of delegitimization.

Being stateless, Rohingya often make headlines due to the constant discrimination, violence, and persecution they face in Myanmar. These attacks have increased in recent years, even in some cases from Buddhist monks, as was the case in 2012. Many have attempted to escape to neighbouring countries, while others have pursued the perilous option of fleeing over the sea. Simultaneous to the current refugee crisis in Europe, the fate of Rohingya boat people stranded at sea has made headlines in Asian media: fleeing persecution in their native land, thousands chose to embark on an uncertain fate, taking maritime routes on makeshift boats. Several Southeast Asian countries have refused to accept them as refugees; and if it were not for the commitment of local fishermen and human rights groups, many more of these uprooted Rohingya people would have perished at sea.

Rohingya live in legal limbo in Myanmar: because of their lack of citizenship, they are denied access to such basic human rights as health and education. Facing constant stigmatization and marginalization in every aspect of their daily lives, they prefer to risk perilous routes abroad in search of a better future for themselves and their children.

Lack of nationality can also be an excuse for a government to expel denationalized persons. For instance, in the case of stateless Dominicans of Haitian descent, Human Rights Watch (HRW) reports that in June 2015, the "military and immigration authorities have repeatedly profiled Dominicans of Haitian descent, detaining and forcibly expelling them, even when they possess valid Dominican documentation."[3]

> Since June, tens of thousands of Haitian migrants and Dominicans of Haitian descent have left the Dominican Republic for Haiti in both forced and "voluntary" departures. The expulsions followed the expiration of a

key deadline in what the Dominican government bills as a plan to give legal status to recent migrants and to restore the nationality of Dominicans of Haitian descent who had been denied their citizenship through a complicated legal and political drama.[4]

The situation in the Dominican Republic is not an isolated case. History has shown us that expulsion of denationalized persons has been used by states as a tool to meet their xenophobic policies of cleansing their population. For instance, thousands of denationalized Jews under the Nazi regime were expelled from their country of birth and forced to resettle in other countries.

Statelessness: A Consequence of Displacement

As well as being a cause for displacement, statelessness can also be a product of migration. Nationality legislations differ from one country to another, for it is primarily states' prerogative to determine the modalities by which they choose to confer nationality on their citizens. With increasing international migration, and particularly forced migration across international borders, the number of children born today from mixed marriages, or in a country that is not the country where their parents are originally from, is on the rise. Consequently, these children may find themselves with either multiple nationalities if they are fortunate, or otherwise with no nationality at all. Statelessness in such cases is therefore a direct consequence of migration, translating into gaps in conflicting nationality laws.

In terms of forced migration, statelessness can result from cases of protracted refugee situations where individuals have fled without proof of nationality – because the identity documents were lost, damaged, or confiscated. After living as refugees abroad for a prolonged period of time, these people will face great difficulties when trying to prove their nationality and return to their country of origin. Children born in such refugee conditions are particularly vulnerable and require special attention.

In some countries, migrants can become stateless because their nationality has been withdrawn by the government due to living abroad for too long. "For example, Article 16 of the Myanmar citizenship law allows for loss of citizenship for any 'citizen who leaves the state permanently.' Although it is unclear how to determine whether an individual has permanently left, the legislation has potential for misuse against forcibly displaced populations."[5] Another example is Article 13 (c) of the Haitian Constitution, which stipulates that one of the conditions for losing Haitian nationality is the "continuous residence abroad of a naturalized Haitian without duly granted authorization by a competent official. Anyone who loses his nationality in this manner may not reacquire it."

The rationale behind this type of restrictive nationality law is the presumed lack of connection, according to the state, between the citizen living abroad and their country of birth. The state considers that such nationals, as a result of their prolonged absence, have renounced their nationality: they are detached from the national affairs of the state and have become citizens of the country they are residing in. Such nationals perceive this as a withdrawal of citizenship by the state.

As we have seen in the previous chapter, the risk of statelessness can also be the result of the lack of birth registration in migration settings. This is particularly the case when nationality laws in both countries restrictively favour the father, thereby paving the way for new cases of statelessness when the father is absent or dead. One illustration is the case of Syrian refugee children born in displacement without the presence of their father. In such cases, "many female-headed households who cannot prove paternity may face difficulties ensuring their newborns obtain nationality."[6]

The absence of birth registration before or during displacement can create complications when trying to document children, particularly if they are unaccompanied minors or foundlings with little or no information about identity or nationality. In addition to experiencing the difficult and precarious conditions of uprootedness, having no indication of their nationality means that these children are or risk becoming stateless.

Risk of Statelessness and Climate-Induced Displacement

With the rising level of the sea resulting from the impact of climate change, several low-lying islands, such as the Maldives, Kiribati, and Tuvalu, risk completely disappearing in a few decades, or even sooner. What will be the fate of entire populations who will be uprooted from their native land because their island has disappeared? Even if some of these islands are not completely submerged by the sea, most will become hostile living environments, lacking cultivable land, drinkable water, etc.

Although we have considered statelessness thus far as the result of state action or inaction (that is, deprivation of nationality, discrimination, conflict of nationality laws, state succession, etc.), climate change will be a completely new factor leading to a potential lack of nationality. The question here is whether the physical territory of a state is the prime element of statehood. In other words, when the state ceases to physically exist, will the nationals also automatically cease being citizens of the state?

Customary international law, as well as the 1933 Montevideo Convention on Rights and Duties of States (Article 1), recognizes that "the state as a person of international law should possess the following qualifications: a) a permanent population; b) a defined territory; c) government; and d) capacity to enter into relations with the other states." Several studies have been done on the potential risk of statelessness of climate-displaced people whose land will cease to exist.[7] This is a scenario that may soon become a reality in the coming years or decades. Since we are still in the upstream phase, it is important to reflect further on how to prevent in a timely manner potential cases of climate-induced statelessness as a result of climate-related uprootedness.

It is to be hoped that discussions and reflections on how to address and prevent the risk of statelessness resulting from climate-induced displacement will continue in the coming years. For instance, a 2011 UNHCR policy research paper suggests,

> One option to prevent statelessness would be for other States to cede territory to the affected State for its continued existence. Full cession of sovereignty over certain territory would be required in such a case. Additionally, in such a situation, other States would have to agree that it is the same State establishing itself in a new territory. In such case, the population could maintain its nationality and would not be rendered stateless. . . . Another option would be to establish a union with another State. Such a union could result in the creation of a new State or lead to one State being subsumed into an existing State. In either scenario the establishment of a federation or a confederation would be possible. . . . The 1961 Convention

provides that in the absence of a treaty specifying otherwise, citizens of the predecessor State should acquire the nationality of the successor State if they would become stateless otherwise.[8]

With the rapidly increasing rising sea level, a solution will hopefully be found for entire populations that will be forced into exile in search of a land in which to live as a community that can retain its traditions and culture.

Increased Vulnerability of Displaced Stateless Persons

Displacement is a challenging journey: individuals and their families are tossed from place to place, sometimes even smuggled across borders, in search of safety or better opportunities. With all of this turmoil and instability, families can be separated and minors left unaccompanied. Statelessness thus exacerbates a situation that is already complex and challenging. This is particularly true when stateless irregular migrants are detained in immigration centres by local authorities.

Arbitrary detention of stateless people

The immigration detention of stateless persons is one of the silent tragedies of our globalised world that plays out behind closed doors, away from the gaze of the media, but with significant, irreparable human cost. It is a tragedy that is completely preventable, but due to a lack of will and attention, continues to harm thousands of lives all around the world every year.[9]

– François Crépeau, UN special rapporteur on the human rights of migrants

As part of their sovereign right, states have the prerogative to determine the criteria regulating the entry, residence, or expulsion of non-nationals from their territory. Similar to voting rights, the right to enter and remain in a country is, in most cases, primarily reserved for nationals.

Because they have no documents, stateless persons can easily find themselves in irregular situations when attempting to cross any border. This can happen even in the country where they were born and have always lived, especially if they have been perceived and labelled as foreigners, non-nationals or outsiders. The immigration status of stateless people is precarious because they do not have the right to travel abroad or, in some cases, to remain within any state. In such scenarios, they often end up in immigration detention centres.

Immigration detention is an administrative incarceration that governments use to achieve administrative objectives such as deportation or the prevention of unlawful entry or residence. Migrants confined in such detention centers are not "illegal" – they are not criminals. Rather, they are detained for an administrative infraction – that is, for crossing the border without proper documents – and are referred to as "irregular" or "undocumented" migrants.

Stateless persons in immigration detention facilities have no country to which to return, and thus there is no country to which the state can deport them. As a result, they risk being detained for long periods of time waiting for their cases to be resolved. A stateless person who is caught attempting to cross a border will be detained as an irregular migrant for illegal entry, since they have no document proving their identity or country of residence. The authorities will place this individual in an immigration detention centre until the state is successful in identifying a country to which they can be deported or resettled.

The story of Khumbulani Frederik Ngubane, a stateless man in South Africa, illustrates this scenario. Frederick was born in 1990 in Newcastle, South Africa. In 1994, he moved with his mother to Kenya. When his mother was murdered, he moved to Uganda with his family. In 2007, he tried to claim his South African citizenship. To do that, he tried to locate some of his mother's relatives in South Africa, but as he was approaching Newcastle, he was arrested for the first time because he had no legal document. He was detained for nearly a month and then sent to a repatriation centre in Lindela. Because there was no consulate or embassy that could recognize him as a citizen, he spent more than 19 months in detention. In a video screened at the First Global Forum on Statelessness in the Hague (15-17 September 2014), Frederick tells his story:

> I had been arrested many times, I cannot even count how many times. Every time I am arrested, I am assaulted. They can kick you, they can hit you . . . They can do anything they want because you don't have any rights. . . . These arrests . . . I don't think it's going to stop. Every time I'm being asked to identify myself, I cannot. . . . People cannot believe that on this planet there are stateless people. But I do exist: I am a stateless person. . . . I end up being like ... nobody. Because I am stateless.[10]

Statelessness thus poses a serious challenge to migration not only because of the absence of identity and travel documents to cross any border, but also because there is no country to which a migrant stateless person has the right to return. Many cases of detention of stateless people go unresolved and underreported. Detained stateless persons, like Frederick, can find themselves in a state of uncertainty, remaining trapped indefinitely in detention until the state detaining them finally resolves their case – either by finding the country in which they used to reside (repatriation), or locating a state that is willing to accept them (resettlement). Stateless persons may find themselves lingering in detention facilities for years because their country of origin refuses to re-admit them in the absence of evidence of their nationality, and the country of detention refuses to release them without proper documentation.

The issue of prolonged or indefinite detention is a serious challenge. It is a threat to the human rights of stateless detainees. As the Equal Rights Trust asserts,

> The administrative purpose behind the detention should be pursued with due diligence throughout the detention period, in order to ensure that detention does not become arbitrary at any stage. Detention should be subject to automatic, regular and periodic review throughout the period of detention, before a judicial body independent of the detaining authorities.[11]

The legality of any immigration detention should be linked to regular review by courts or a competent administrative body. Detention for immigration purposes should be proportionate, a last resort, and necessary. It should be respectful of the basic and fundamental human rights of the immigration detainees. Indefinite, prolonged or repeated detention of migrants, whether they are stateless or not, would amount to a serious violation of their basic human rights.

Prolonged or repeated detention can cause serious psychological distress and a sense of hopelessness for individuals. These people will feel they are being punished for being stateless, which is a status they did not ask for but have to live with. Stateless persons in immigration detention are therefore vulnerable on all levels, as "without the full set of rights available to citizens, stateless persons face a greater likelihood of discrimination in the administration of justice, harassment and arbitrary detention. One common problem faced by stateless persons – as also by IDPs – is a lack of documentation which can leave them more vulnerable to rights violations."[12] This is particularly the case for women, children, and unaccompanied minors,

As the case of stateless detainees is quite exceptional, states should look into alternative measures to detention. They should try their best to come up with non-coercive solutions that will preserve and respect the human rights and human dignity of the detainees. Stateless persons in detention are not criminals: they are held for an administrative infraction – that is, irregular entry or presence in the territory – and should be treated with dignity. Many are fleeing from persecution, harassment, or discrimination from the place they called "home." Condemning them to prolonged or repeated detention is another stumbling block for them to deal with, and one that further victimizes them.

Trafficked stateless persons: invisible twice

Human trafficking is another challenge to which stateless persons risk being exposed. Human trafficking is a lucrative form of organized crime that generates billions of dollars every day. Although the terms "smuggling" and "human trafficking" are sometimes interchangeably used, these are different concepts with different implications for the individuals. Let us first look at their meaning and differences.

The UN Protocol against the Smuggling of Migrants by Land, Sea and Air (Article 3.a) defines smuggling as "the procurement, in order to obtain, directly or indirectly, a financial or other material benefit, of the illegal entry of a person into a state Party of which the person is not a national or a permanent resident." Smuggling therefore involves consent, that is, a mutual financial agreement between the smuggler and the migrant, to transport the person across an international border through irregular means. This can be done, for example, by providing forged passports, or by arranging transportation through routes with little or no immigration control.

With regard to human trafficking, the UN Protocol to Prevent, Suppress and Punish Trafficking in Persons, Especially Women and Children (Article 3.a) offers the following definition:

"Trafficking in persons" shall mean the recruitment, transportation, transfer, harbouring or receipt of persons, by means of the threat or use of force or other forms of coercion, of abduction, of fraud, of deception, of the abuse of power or of a position of vulnerability or of the giving or receiving of payments or benefits to achieve the consent of a person having control over another person, for the purpose of exploitation. Exploitation shall include, at a minimum, the exploitation of the prostitution of others or other forms of sexual exploitation, forced labour or services, slavery or practices similar to slavery, servitude or the removal of organs.[13]

Human trafficking is a modern form of slavery. It involves coercion, exploitation, deceit, and fraud for the purpose of making money through the commodification and selling of human beings. It is a violation of basic human rights and can occur across or within borders. Human trafficking is a risk to which stateless people are vulnerable.

The main differences between smuggling and trafficking are therefore consent and exploitation. While the smuggled person agrees to being taken abroad clandestinely, a trafficked person has not given consent or has been lured into agreeing through false promises with the premeditated end result of exploiting the victim. And while the illicit transaction between the smuggler and the migrant ends upon arrival in the destination country, victims of trafficking are exploited at the final destination, and sometimes also during the journey.

Despite these major differences, the line between smuggling and human trafficking can sometimes be blurred in situations where smuggled persons themselves become victims of human trafficking at some point in the smuggling process. In other words, although smuggled persons can become victims of human trafficking, all smuggling does not necessarily lead to trafficking. One example of such blurred lines is the case of Rohingya Muslims resorting to smugglers in attempting to flee into Malaysia, with tragic results:

> On May 1, 2015, a joint military-police taskforce discovered at least 30 bodies at an abandoned human trafficking camp in the Sadao district of Songkhla province close to the Thai-Malaysian border. Many were buried in shallow graves, while others were covered with blankets and clothes and left in the open. Police reports indicate the dead are ethnic Rohingya Muslims from Burma and Bangladesh who starved to death or died of disease while held by traffickers who were awaiting payment of ransoms before smuggling them into Malaysia. Traffickers controlling this camp apparently departed into the mountainous jungle, taking surviving Rohingya with them.[14]

Facing constant marginalization and discrimination in their country of origin, stateless persons resort to smugglers to cross borders and seek better opportunities abroad. Since they have no documents proving their names or nationalities, they are easy prey for unscrupulous traffickers, who will lure them with the promise of a better life or a well-paid job somewhere else, abroad or within the country, and then exploit them. Although there is no causal link between statelessness and human trafficking, it remains the case that stateless persons are at great risk of being exploited.

Deceitful traffickers often confiscate, steal, or destroy their victims' documents, either on arrival in the destination country or prior to transfer. Consequently, victims are unable to prove their identity when they try to return to their country of origin. Without any trace or proof of their existence, stateless people are already "invisible" in the eyes of the law. When they become victims of human trafficking, stateless persons become even more untraceable: they become "invisible" twice.

The fact that victims have no documentation also means that the state has no information about their identity, that is, their name, age, or country of origin. This makes it difficult for authorities to properly investigate cases of trafficking or prosecute traffickers. On the other side, victims of trafficking in many cases are unaware of their rights, and are afraid or reluctant to go to local authorities to assert their rights.

Stateless women and children, particularly girls, are especially vulnerable. During the 2011 Commission of the Churches on International Affairs (CCIA) visit to the Cox

Bazaar area in Bangladesh, the delegation had the chance to talk to Rohingya living in the Kutupalong and Nayapara makeshift camps, and were disturbed to learn that women and girls who have no legal evidence of their existence are often abducted by traffickers, who smuggle them abroad for exploitation. According to the WCC Statement on the Human Rights of Stateless People, "The lack of documentation also makes Rohingya women and girls particularly vulnerable to physical attacks, sexual violence and trafficking."[15] Victims can end up in domestic servitude, agricultural work, the sex trade industry, or be forced into child labour.

As a fellowship of churches, how can our constituency deal with these issues of statelessness? How should we go about it? What are the tools at our disposal to address this pressing concern? The next chapter will grapple with these questions.

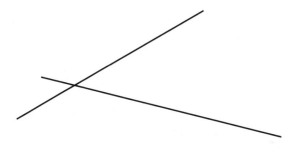

5. The Way Forward

This chapter will consider some theological precepts that could inspire and encourage churches and the ecumenical family at large, in collaboration with sister faiths and other relevant actors, to embrace and address the issue of statelessness. It will also examine possible avenues for churches and religious communities to contribute to and collaborate with partners, such as the UNHCR, and international processes such as the Sustainable Development Goals.

Theological Grounding and Pilgrimage of Justice and Peace

Speak out for those who cannot speak,
for the rights of all the destitute.

Speak out, judge righteously,
defend the rights of the poor and needy.
– Proverbs 31:8-9

God is on the side of the poor, the marginalized, the excluded
– those who are discriminated against. God is for them, and
with them. As we fulfil God's reign on earth, our responsibility as Christians and as churches is to side with those
who are vulnerable, forgotten. It becomes therefore obvious
that WCC member churches are called to side with stateless
people and their communities wherever they are found, irrespective of their race or religious affiliation. Stateless people
are "expected to stay alive without security, be human without dignity, harvest a land no longer theirs, and feed their
children from empty plates. They are the unseen real who fill
the earth: the 'no people' with 'no tomorrow' to whom Jesus
announced an emphatic 'yes'."[1]

Our Lord Jesus cared for the marginalized, those who
are isolated from community and stigmatized by society. It
is our vocation and calling as a fellowship of churches to be
sensible to the plight and hardship that stateless people experience, to care and protect them. It is therefore our mission
to be prophetic and denounce the plight of stateless people,
to advocate for their rights and their place in the world, to
care for their needs, and to pursue justice with them or on
their behalf.

Statelessness is one of the many signs that we live in a broken world, in which the worth and dignity of human beings are threatened. In order to heal this brokenness, the prophetic role of churches requires faith leaders to speak the truth into our lives. Religious leaders have a responsibility to speak and act for the truth, to denounce the flaws of our broken world, and to exhort those around them to strive for the protection and respect of all human beings, for we are all made in the image of God:

> Then God said, "Let us make humankind in our image, according to our likeness; and let them have dominion over the fish of the sea, and over the birds of the air, and over the cattle, and over all the wild animals of the earth, and over every creeping thing that creeps upon the earth."
> So God created humankind in his image,
> in the image of God he created them;
> male and female he created them. (Gen. 1:26-27)

The image of God, while it can never be fulfilled in an individual who chooses to be closed off from God or from the other, can never be effaced from any person. In many circumstances the Church will rightly defend the cause or dignity of one person against the antagonism or prejudice of a whole society, recognising that the least or most isolated individual is infinitely precious in the sight of God.[2]

Churches and faith communities do not live in isolation from the world. They are an integral part of the community and the society, and are thereby equally affected by the struggles and challenges of members of the community, including stateless persons. "For as in one body we have many members, and not all the members have the same function, so we, who are many, are one body in Christ, and individually we are members one of another" (Rom. 12:4-5).

With regard to stateless people and their communities, churches are called to carry out their prophetic and compassionate ministry which often implies speaking truth and justice to power, denouncing and standing against every form of injustice, oppression and conflict, and more than ever challenging the leaders of society. It is their responsibility to stand by the side of the disadvantaged, the forgotten, the excluded, and to give voice to their concerns, challenges, and plight. As stated in the WCC publication *The Church: Towards a Common Vision:*

> Jesus said that he came so that human beings may have life in abundance (cf. John 10:10); his followers acknowledge their responsibility to defend human life and dignity. These are obligations on churches as much as on individual believers. . . . Christians will seek to promote the values of the kingdom of God by working together with adherents of other religions and even with those of no religious belief. [3]

As Christians, we are called to be the "salt of the earth" and the "light of the world" (Matt. 5:13-16). This is an exhortation to heal and redress broken relationships, decry and resist injustice, raise awareness about the plight of those oppressed and experiencing injustice, engage with authorities to plead for the respect and dignity of stateless people experiencing hardship. It is also a call for transformation at the personal and communal levels.

These biblical and theological bases motivate us as churches and Christian bodies to express our Christian commitment and to be engaged in our prophetic witness to speak for the rights of those who are voiceless and marginalized as stateless people. The Christian family, therefore, ought to take up the plight of stateless persons as this struggle reflects our cardinal universal principles and values: that a human being has the right to life, liberty and security; the right to education, equal protection under the law, and to be free from slavery and torture; the right to freedom of thought, conscience, and religion, and to freedom of opinion and expression; and the right to a nationality. Stateless persons are denied all of these rights and are unrecognized by any nation.[4]

Churches and the ecumenical family should not remain indifferent or insensible when human rights are violated, communities persecuted, human beings discriminated against. They are called to play a meaningful role by engaging governments to reform their nationality laws in order to prevent new cases of statelessness from arising as well as by address existing (and protracted) cases of statelessness. "In this way Christians are able to stand in the tradition of the prophets who proclaimed God's judgment on all injustice."[5]

WCC Pilgrimage of Justice and Peace

A Pilgrimage of Justice and Peace must mean that we should pray that God leads us to any place where justice and peace are threatened, be they in countries of conflict or in relationships of oppression and injustices across borders. We should go to these places, not out of curiosity, but through our true and honest willingness to be in solidarity and do something to bring justice and peace.[6]
– Olav F. Tveit, *Ecumenical Review*, July 2014.

During the WCC's 10th Assembly in Busan, Republic of Korea, the ecumenical family embarked on a Pilgrimage of Justice and Peace. This ecumenical journey is an invitation to churches of the ecumenical family at large to become instruments of justice and peace through God's transforming and healing grace. As Christians, we are called to promote and stand for just and peaceful community where everyone's rights and dignity are respected and upheld. "The pilgrimage takes place in a world that cries out for engagement by

Christians and all people of good will. . . . This pilgrimage will lead us to the locations of ugly violence and injustices. We intend to look for God's incarnated presence in the midst of suffering, exclusion, and discrimination."[7]

The Pilgrimage is an appeal for tangible actions of transformation: "This will include the strength to resist evil – injustice and violence, even if a church finds itself in a minority situation. . . . The credibility of our actions might grow from the quality of the fellowship we share – a fellowship of justice and peace."[8]

In the context of stateless people, the Pilgrimage is an invitation for churches and the ecumenical family to meet God "wherever people suffer injustice, violence and war. To experience God's presence with the most vulnerable, the wounded, and the marginalized is a transformative experience"[9] As Christians and as churches, we are called to work for the transformation of an unjust world that is excluding stateless people. We can do this through engaging state authorities to ensure that all individuals enjoy the fundamental right to nationality, as well as by caring for and protecting stateless people. Churches' diaconal work, that is, their service and care to ensure human dignity for all, should therefore involve prophetic witness. As part of their prophetic *diakonia*, local congregations are the best placed to care for stateless people, voice their concern, and include them in the community of pilgrims.

As respected moral authorities, churches can also play a pivotal role in tackling statelessness by entering into dialogue with their respective governments. We can urge them to make the necessary changes in their nationality laws to prevent further cases of statelessness from arising, thereby resolving protracted situations of statelessness.

The Pilgrimage is also a call "to look for God´s incarnated presence in the midst of suffering, exclusion, and discrimination,"[10] to witness together as an ecumenical family, and to advocate for justice and peace. In the context of statelessness, this implies that church leaders are invited to encourage governments to adopt national legislation that will ensure that no one is arbitrarily stripped of his or her nationality, that women and men stand on equal footing when it comes to nationality laws, and that children are protected from the risk of being born stateless. Resolving cases of statelessness will inevitably lead to a more stable, peaceful, and developed country.

The Pilgrimage of Justice and Peace is an invitation to be prophetic and to voice the concerns of the marginalized, the forgotten people. Being church involves speaking to the concerns and plight of those who are oppressed, as well as those who are "invisible" in society. It is about bringing those who have been left on the margins of society to the centre of debate and discussion. Stateless people live among us, within our communities. Because churches and religious groups are present even in the most remote areas, they are primary agents in providing sanctuary and protection for those who are persecuted, to stand by their side and uphold their rights and dignity.

The Pilgrimage invites the ecumenical family to walk together and work in collaboration with religious communities, states, civil society, international organizations, academics, and experts. This collaboration includes working with the people concerned, that is, stateless persons, and making sure they are made "visible": churches should work with stateless persons to ensure their voices are heard.

UNHCR Campaign to End Statelessness

One way to connect the Pilgrimage of Justice and Peace to the issue of statelessness issues is through collaboration with the UNHCR in its ten-year global action plan to end statelessness by 2024. As part of its mandate, the UNHCR is in charge of preventing and reducing statelessness in the world. It also works to ensure that the human rights of stateless persons are respected and protected, and it helps establish procedures by which stateless persons can be identified.

On the occasion of the 60th Anniversary of the 1954 Convention relating to the Status of Stateless Persons, during the First Global Forum on Statelessness organized by UNHCR, in collaboration with Tilburg University, at the Peace Palace in the Hague (15–17 September 2014), the UNHCR launched a ten-year campaign.[11] The campaign proposes a global and holistic strategy to prevent and eradicate statelessness articulated in ten actions:

Action 1: Resolve existing major situations of statelessness.

Action 2: Ensure that no child is born stateless.

Action 3: Remove gender discrimination from nationality laws.

Action 4: Prevent denial, loss, or deprivation of nationality on discriminatory grounds.

Action 5: Prevent statelessness in cases of state succession.

Action 6: Grant protection status to stateless migrants and facilitate their naturalization.

Action 7: Ensure birth registration for the prevention of statelessness.

Action 8: Issue nationality documentation to those with entitlement to it.

Action 9: Accede to the UN Statelessness Conventions.

Action 10: Improve quantitative and qualitative data on stateless populations.

It should be noted that the actions are not listed in terms of relevance or priority. Furthermore, since the causes and scale of statelessness vary from one country to the other, not all of these actions will apply to all cases of statelessness. Depending on the context, one or more actions can be identified to solve existing cases of statelessness, or to prevent new cases from arising. Once the relevant actions are identified, National Action Plans will be developed at the country level in order to determine strategies, goals, and milestones for the fulfillment and achievement of the actions.

To ensure the success of this campaign, the UNHCR is working collaboratively with all partners, including other UN agencies, civil society, and scholars, as well as faith-based organizations and religious communities. UNHCR collaboration with the faith community was the subject of the UNHCR High Commissioner's 5th Dialogue on Protection Challenges, which took place 12–13 December 2012 in Geneva, Switzerland, on the theme "Faith and Protection." With regard to issues of statelessness, this dialogue marked the beginning of a fruitful collaboration between the WCC/CCIA and UNHCR Statelessness Unit. In the spirit of this collaboration, which is in line with the idea of "walking together" in WCC's Pilgrimage of Justice and Peace, churches and the ecumenical family are encouraged to contribute to preventing and eradicating statelessness in our respective contexts.

In practical terms, such collaboration would for instance mean that churches and church-related organizations contribute to the national consultation process with UNHCR, national institutions, and all other relevant partners in developing and implementing the National Action Plans (NAP), as well as periodically reporting on the fulfillment of the goals and objectives set out in the NAP. As churches and religious communities are part of the grassroots of society, their first-hand experience with stateless persons will greatly benefit the consultative process, ensuring that the NAP accurately incorporates and highlights the human dimension of statelessness. Faith communities can either collaborate in the proceedings or initiate the process in collaboration with all partners in order to bring all stakeholders to the same table, including representatives of the affected communities, and start a constructive dialogue.

The collaboration between UNHCR and faith communities at large can also lead to identifying new cases of statelessness. In many countries, stateless persons hide from authorities out of fear of being detained or expelled. They often are not included in national censuses, either because they are forgotten or ignored, or because they are hiding in fear of being deported and therefore remain "invisible." Such partnership can more accurately gauge the scale and location of statelessness in the country, as well as the cause and impact. Acting as a place of safety, churches and other religious groups can provide a more precise picture of the magnitude of statelessness, as well as the profile of the affected persons. With such information, national authorities will be better equipped to map and prevent new cases of statelessness from emerging, as well to find durable solutions for existing or protracted cases.

Raising awareness about statelessness is another essential area of cooperation. Being legally "invisible," stateless people often live among us without our knowledge. Some might hide their lack of legal status to avoid being stigmatized by members of society or ill-treated by authorities. The Pilgrimage of Justice and Peace invites us to be prophetic and denounce injustice. In that spirit, churches and religious communities can join their voices with those of partners engaged in UNHCR campaign to raise awareness about the plight of stateless people and the obstacles they face constantly. We can engage with relevant governmental authorities to address the human rights violations these people experience. Unity is strength after all.

Knowledge is power. In collaboration with UNHCR and other stakeholders, churches and church-related groups can educate and inform stateless people about their rights. Because they fear being arrested or deported, many of them live in hiding, thus increasing their vulnerability and marginalization. Despite their lack of legal status, though, stateless persons are entitled to basic and fundamental human rights, including the right to life, to health care, to adequate housing, to education, and to move freely within a country. Churches and partners can explore the possibility of organizing training workshops specifically designed to educate and empower stateless persons and their communities. They can also consider producing pamphlets listing the rights to which stateless persons are entitled and indicating the various types of procedures and other avenues at their disposal. Once they are informed of their rights, stateless persons will be able to assert them and contribute meaningfully to the society in which they live.

Churches and church-related groups can also provide practical assistance to stateless persons by helping them fill out the applications forms for their nationality documentation and birth registration. Illiteracy can be prevalent among stateless people living in the margins of society. Many are unaware of their rights and of administrative procedures they have to go through to secure necessary documents to prove their legal identity.

Churches and faith communities can also benefit from UNHCR's technical advice, for instance, in terms of protecting women in mixed marriages from unwanted changes in nationality that could in the long run render them stateless, or protecting stateless persons in irregular situations from being detained indefinitely in immigration centres. We can also seek legal advice to determine the nationality of foundlings, or to uphold the right to birth registration for all children, irrespective of the status or nationality of their parents. Such support can include facilitating access to legal clinics, or deploying itinerant judicial hearings to establish birth certificates.

In countries where nationality laws do not treat women and men equally, churches and religious communities can work with UNHCR in engaging the government to reform these discriminatory laws: for example, by allowing women to pass their nationality to and register their children. Faith communities in particular can play an important role in engaging members of congregations and changing cultural and traditional misconceptions about the role of women in society, reminding people that men and women are both created in the image of God. Since time immemorial, faith communities have been considered the moral authorities, and have in this way helped write history by influencing policies. Churches can make it their mission to uphold and strengthen the place of women in society by recognizing their equal worth and contribution. Ensuring gender equality in nationality laws is an attainable and realistic objective, particularly when met with good will and commitment.

Prison ministry is another important expression and dimension of churches' presence in the midst of those who are suffering. In addition to the constant rejection and discrimination stateless persons can face, detention can be a gruelling experience, as it adds a sense of despair and disenfranchisement. Although immigration detention is a type of administrative incarceration, stateless immigration detainees can feel they are treated like criminals. Chaplains can play an important role in visiting and bringing spiritual comfort to stateless persons who are detained in immigration detention centres, at times for prolonged periods of time. They can reach out to stateless detainees and become a fortifying presence, a spiritual support. They can listen to their stories and even bring their cases to the relevant authorities, or to the attention of the media.

Finally, inter-religious collaboration can play a vital role in bringing a meaningful and lasting response to statelessness in various contexts. Religious diversity is common in almost all countries in the world today. Solutions therefore have to be found through dialogue and collaboration with sister faiths, "respecting the reality of other religious traditions and affirming their distinctiveness and identity."[12]

Den Dolder Recommendations

Prior to the 2014 Global Forum on Statelessness, the WCC/CCIA and Kerk in Actie organized an international ecumenical consultation with participants from Africa, Asia, the Caribbean, Europe, and North America. The consultation – held in September 2014 in Den Dolder, the Netherlands – also benefited from the input of several stateless persons. The aim of the event was to prepare for the Global Forum and articulate basic recommendations that would serve as guidelines for WCC member churches and the ecumenical family at large when taking action on statelessness issues. During the Global Forum, UNHCR provided space for the WCC delegation to read the recommendations, known as the "Den Dolder Recommendations,[13] to the participants of the forum, as a sign of the on-going collaboration between the WCC and UNHCR.

The document starts by affirming our inherent dignity, worth, and equality as human beings, since we have all been created in the image of God. It then reminds us that "nations, nationality and citizenship are human constructs" which "should always promote human rights, not detract from them." As human beings, we are all entitled to basic human rights, including the right to a nationality. It is therefore our "common responsibility to prevent and end statelessness and to protect stateless people."

Recalling that "solidarity and compassion" are signs of "Christian discipleship," the Den Dolder document recommends several actions that churches and the ecumenical family could consider in their efforts to end statelessness. For instance, churches and church-related groups can address the discrimination and marginalization that stateless persons experience by protecting them and helping them "become full and equal members of the community." This entails denouncing the injustice that stateless people face, assisting them to have their rights recognized, and giving them a voice to share their plight.

Churches can also encourage their respective governments to sign and ratify both the 1954 and 1961 UN Statelessness Conventions. Ratification and implementation of these instruments, as well as other international human rights treaties, are the first steps to securing a safe and solid human rights framework that could ensure rights to all.

With regard to childhood statelessness, churches are encouraged to put "an end to the statelessness of children by 2019, the midpoint of the UN decade" by promoting universal birth registration; launching the ecumenical campaign, No Child Should Be Stateless!; and calling "for an end to gender discrimination in nationality laws."

The Den Dolder Recommendations also assert the role of churches in registering important life events "such as birth, baptism, confirmation, marriage, and death – in ways that help people to secure documents that help reduce statelessness." If national authorities and faith communities are willing to collaborate, baptismal records are certainly very useful when it comes to obtaining birth certificates for stateless persons.

Sustainable Development Goals (SDGs)

We are determined to take the bold and transformative steps which are urgently needed to shift the world on to a sustainable and resilient path. As we embark on this collective journey, we pledge that no one will be left behind.

— Preamble of the 2030 Agenda for Sustainable Development

As a successor to the Millennium Development Goals, scheduled to end in December 2015, the Sustainable Development Goals (SDGs) were adopted on 25 September 2015 by member states of the UN during its Sustainable Development Summit in New York, US. The SDGs constitute an open invitation to states, the UN and its agencies, civil society, faith-based organizations and faith communities, the academic world, and all possible stakeholders to work in "collaborative partnership" and take "bold and transformative steps which are urgently needed to shift the world onto a sustainable and resilient path."[14]

During the summit, states agreed on a set of 17 goals, composed of 169 specific targets, to be achieved by 2030:

1. End poverty in all its forms everywhere
2. End hunger, achieve food security and improved nutrition, and promote sustainable agriculture
3. Ensure healthy lives and promote wellbeing for all at all ages
4. Ensure inclusive and equitable quality education and promote life-long learning opportunities for all

5. Achieve gender equality and empower all women and girls

6. Ensure availability and sustainable management of water and sanitation for all

7. Ensure access to affordable, reliable, sustainable, and modern energy for all

8. Promote sustained, inclusive, and sustainable economic growth; full and productive employment; and decent work for all

9. Build resilient infrastructure, promote inclusive and sustainable industrialization, and foster innovation

10. Reduce inequality within and among countries

11. Make cities and human settlements inclusive, safe, resilient, and sustainable

12. Ensure sustainable consumption and production patterns

13. Take urgent action to combat climate change and its impacts

14. Conserve and sustainably use the oceans, seas and marine resources for sustainable development

15. Protect, restore, and promote sustainable use of terrestrial ecosystems; sustainably manage forests; combat desertification; halt and reverse land degradation, and halt biodiversity loss

16. Promote peaceful and inclusive societies for sustainable development; provide access to justice for all;

and build effective, accountable, and inclusive institutions at all levels

17. Strengthen the means of implementation and revitalize the global partnership for sustainable development

The SDGs, enshrined in the 2030 Agenda for Sustainable Development (2030 Agenda), seek to build on the MDGs and go further by upholding human rights for all as an essential element of development.

> The worlds of "human rights" and "development" have for many decades run parallel to each other, blindingly indifferent to the complementarity of their objectives, the overlap of principles they foster and the near impossibleness of achieving one without the other. Thus, where in an ideal world there would have been healthy cross-fertilisation between the two fields – a wholesome marriage resulting in the offspring of justice, prosperity and sustainability – we have experienced polarisation, territorialism, contradiction and competition for resources between the two, to the extent that there are very few people who can genuinely claim real expertise in both fields, and even fewer examples of real success in both grounds.[15]

The SDGs mark a new dawn with the acknowledgment that human rights are essential to and linked with sustainable development. In addition to their social, economic, and environmental objectives, the SDGs cover a wide set of human rights, including social, cultural, political, economic, and civil rights, and they strive for "peaceful, just and inclusive societies":

> We envisage a world of universal respect for human rights and human dignity, the rule of law, justice, equality and non-discrimination; of respect for race, ethnicity and cultural diversity; and of equal opportunity permitting the full realization of human potential and contributing to shared prosperity. A world which invests in its children and in which every child grows up free from violence and exploitation. A world in which every woman and girl enjoys full gender equality and all legal, social and economic barriers to their empowerment have been removed. A just, equitable, tolerant, open and socially inclusive world in which the needs of the most vulnerable are met.

In addition, the 2030 Agenda is inclusive of the entire human family: in several places the document stresses that "no one will be left behind." The introduction, for example, affirms that "recognising that the dignity of the human person is fundamental, we wish to see the Goals and targets met for all nations and peoples and for all segments of society. And we will endeavour to reach the furthest behind first."[16]

The SDGs therefore explicitly invite governments and all stakeholders to include all individuals in the journey leading to 2030. This includes stateless people as well as non-citizens in general, who should not be excluded or left behind in the process but rather given the opportunity to enjoy the fruits and benefits of development.

Legal identity: A global development issue

In order for SDGs to seriously and effectively take into account stateless persons, states need to include them in their national data. The invisibility of stateless people in terms of national statistics, registries, and other censuses increases their vulnerability. Proof of nationality and birth registration are essential elements of legal identity that would help prevent and address statelessness. Without any trace or proof of their existence, stateless communities can easily find themselves left out of national policy planning or national health-care programmes. Often living in poor economic conditions as a result of discrimination, stateless persons in many countries experience poverty, illiteracy, unemployment, and exploitation as a result of their lack of documentation. If they are not incorporated into national statistics, they will not be in a position to benefit from the developments linked to the SDGs, and will continue to live in precarious conditions.

Hence, for the SDGs to have a meaningful impact on all individuals of any society, we must ensure that statistics and information are as comprehensive, detailed and reliable as possible. This is certainly an area where churches and other faith communities can play an essential role, by making sure that no one in their congregations is left "invisible" with regard to official records. This is also an occasion to strengthen collaboration between churches and other faith-based organizations, governments, civil society, and the UN and its agencies.

Goal 16.9 – which aims to "provide legal identity for all, including birth registration," by 2030[17] – is particularly essential to our discussion on stateless persons. The insertion of this specific goal calls for celebration, because legal documentation is now recognized and addressed as a global development issue. Although we are all entitled to fundamental human rights by virtue of being, in many countries legal identity is a gateway to a wide range of rights, such as health care and education. Legal identity can therefore be seen as a pre-requisite or an enabler for the success and effectiveness of many of the SDGs and their targets. The statistics for civil registrations, and particularly birth registrations, now become indicators for SDG 16.9. Civil registry should be universal, accessible, and free – or at least low-cost. Although the absence of birth registration does not necessarily translate into statelessness, in practice it is in some countries an obstacle for children to access education, health care or other basic facilities.

As we have seen in previous chapters, baptismal records and other forms of religious documents marking important life events can be used to corroborate claims in establishing birth certificates or any other civil registry document. This is certainly an area where churches and religious communities could work hand in hand with national authorities, governments, and other partners. The SDGs therefore represent another avenue for enhanced collaborative work between churches and other faith-based organizations, governments, civil society, and the UN and its agencies. Churches and faith-based communities can play a significant role in strengthening SDGs in their respective contexts.

Combatting statelessness with gender equality

Gender equality is an indispensable element of a peaceful and prosperous world. Unfortunately, in reality discrimination against women and gender inequality persist in legal as well as social settings. Recognizing the central role women play in development, the 2030 Agenda articulates a specific goal dedicated to promoting gender equality: the aim of Goal 5 is to "achieve gender equality and empower all women and girls."

In countries where nationality laws do not give women the same rights as men in terms of conferral of nationality, Goal 5 calls for ending "all forms of discrimination against all women and girls everywhere." Goal 5 also calls for the elimination of violence against women and girls, such as human trafficking and child marriage, and calls for "sound policies and enforceable legislation for the promotion of gender equality and the empowerment of all women and girls at all levels." It is to be hoped that UN Member States that adopted the 2030 Agenda will live up to their commitment and work toward greater equality between women and men in their country.

Conclusion

Although it is a problem that is often hidden and overlooked, statelessness is not just about laws and statistics, but instead is, first and foremost, about individuals, families, and communities. It is a *human* issue, and a human *rights* issue. Its impact lingers in the lives of millions of individuals, often over generations. Beyond its legal and political dimensions, statelessness is primarily a major human and identity issue that deserves more attention than it receives. With no state claiming them as nationals, stateless people are "orphans of nationality,"[18] and are consequently legally "invisible" to any state administration. Lack of nationality is a blatant denial of personhood.

Stateless people long for a place in the world. They primarily seek recognition, simply a trace of their existence under the law. Civil registry documents do not give us a nationality: they evidence our legal existence. Without any form of civil registration – birth, marriage, death, etc. – a person leaves no trace at all that they exist. This seems quite surreal in our present world, where every aspect of our lives is kept in records.

Stateless people are evidence that states are unable to incorporate into their domestic laws the human right to a nationality that is enshrined in international law and international customary law. The presence of millions of stateless persons therefore signals the weakness of international law and is a lacuna of the statehood state system.It is crucial to be reminded that nationality is not a privilege, nor a reward: it is a fundamental human right. Everyone is entitled to it simply by virtue of being human. This right is about state protection, and is not meant to become a weapon of discrimination or persecution. It is therefore important to relentlessly affirm and uphold the right to a nationality for all, as it contributes to human dignity, justice, and peace.

Statelessness is an irregularity, a legal vacuum, an anomaly of the Westphalian state system. With the level of progress made in the fields of human rights, it is unthinkable that in today's world there are individuals, families and communities that do not have any nationality at all. Consequently, these people are denied the very element that would entitle them to a wide range of rights: nationality. The reality is saddening: millions of stateless persons actually live among us, within our societies, and are "invisible," forgotten, clandestine.

The WCC Pilgrimage of Justice and Peace together with the UNHCR campaign to eradicate statelessness and the SDGs are indicators that we are experiencing a critical juncture, a *Kairos* moment. The time is ripe for churches and the ecumenical family, in collaboration with other religious groups and all partners, to stand up and affirm the right of the voiceless, the marginalized, the forgotten, the stateless. Now is the opportune moment to work together, the time for prophetic transformation, inspired and driven by the Holy Spirit.

Churches and religious communities, being at the grassroots of societies, are best placed to protect stateless persons and assist them in times of difficulties. They are also in a position to help in mapping and identifying stateless persons. Religious communities can contribute meaningfully to preventing new cases of statelessness from arising, as well as to finding solutions and reducing existing cases. This publication, as a modest attempt to acquaint readers with the issue of statelessness and its various facets and ramifications, is also an invitation to reflect further on the individual themes of the preceding chapters.

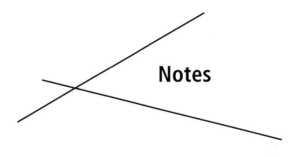

Notes

Chapter 1: Who Is Stateless? Why? Where?

1.   Donald G. McNeil Jr., "Founder of Zambia Is Declared Stateless in High Court Ruling, *New York Times,* 1 April 1999, at: http://www.nytimes.com/1999/04/01/world/founder-of-zambia-is-declared-stateless-in-high-court-ruling.html.

2.   See Matthew J. Gibney, "Statelessness and the Right to Citizenship," *Forced Migration Review* 39 (April 2009), 50.

3.   See Mathews George Chunakara, "Statelessness and Human Rights of Stateless People: An Overview," *Human Rights of Stateless People*, Commission of the Churches on International Affairs (WCC, 2013), 19.

4.   A. Lang and John Williams, *Hannah Arendt and International Relations: Readings across the Lines* (Palgrave Macmillan, 2005), 109.

5.   See Mark Manly, "Statelessness and International Law: An Overview," from *Human Rights of Stateless People*, Commission of the Churches on International Affairs (WCC, 2013), 47.

6.   UN High Commissioner for Refugees (UNHCR), "Statelessness: Hoping to Acquire a Nationality and Put Down Roots," UN Refugee Agency website, 1 September 2014, at: http://www.unhcr.org/5404761a6.html.

7.   See Conny Rijken, Laura van Waas, Martin Gramatikov, and Deirdre Brennan, *The Nexus between Statelessness and Human Trafficking in Thailand* (The Netherlands: Wolf Legal Publishers, 2015), at: http://www.institutesi.org/Stateless-Trafficking_Thailand.pdf. The study explores

potential links between statelessness and human trafficking among hill tribe people in Thailand.

8.   See Laura Van Waas, "Nationality and Rights," in Statelessness and the Benefits of Citizenship: A Comparative Study, ed. Brad K. Blitz and Maureen Lynch (Cheltenham; Northampton, Mass.: Edward Elgar, 2011), 24–25.

9.   UNHCR, *Nationality and Statelessness: A Handbook for Parliamentarians* (Inter-Parliamentary Union with the UNHCR, 2005), 8, at: http://www.ipu.org/pdf/publications/nationality_en.pdf.

10.   UNHCR, "Introductory Note," Convention relating to the Status of Stateless Persons: Text of the 1954 Convention Relating to the Status of Stateless Persons (UNHCR, 2004), 3, at: http://www.unhcr.org/3bbb25729.html.

11.   UNHCR, "Objectives and Key Provisions of the 1954 Convention Relating to the Status of Stateless Persons," UNHCR website, 1 October 2001, at: http://www.unhcr.org/3bd7d3394.html.

Chapter 2: Discriminatory Practices

1.   WCC *Communiqué*, from Human Rights of Stateless People, Commission of the Churches on International Affairs (WCC, 2013), 13.

2.   *Stateless in the Dominican Republic: Dioniso*, YouTube Video, Open Society Foundations, 2009: at: https://www.youtube.com/watch?v=IT-8fuUfW-Bg.

3.   UNHCR, *Stories of Statelessness: Latvia and Estonia*, UNHCR website, at: http://www.unhcr.org/ibelong/stories-of-statelessness-latvia-and-estonia/.

4.   UN, *Report of the Independent Expert on Minority Issues, Gay McDougall*, Human Rights Council 13th session, UN General Assembly, 7 January 2010, 16, at: http://www2.ohchr.org/english/bodies/hrcouncil/docs/13session/A-HRC-13-23.pdf.

5.   See Sarnata Reynolds, "Statelessness and Discrimination," *Human Rights of Stateless People*, Commission of the Churches on International Affairs (WCC, 2013), 40.

6.   Amal de Chickera and Joanna Whiteman, "Discrimination and the Human Security of Stateless People," *Forced Migration Review* 46 (May 2014), 56.

7.   UNHCR, *Background Note on Gender Equality, Nationality Laws and Statelessness 2015*, 6 March 2015, 3, at: http://www.refworld.org/docid/54f8369b4.html.

8.   UN Division for the Advancement of Women, "Women, Nationality and Citizenship," *Women 2000 and Beyond* (June 2003), 5, at: http://www.un.org/womenwatch/daw/public/jun03e.pdf.

9.   *No Nationality, No Future*, YouTube Video, Women's Refugee Commission, 6 June 2013, at: https://www.youtube.com/watch?v=qZ_Y0hW3DdA.

10.   Women's Refugee Commission, *Our Motherland, Our Country: Gender Discrimination and Statelessness in the Middle East and North Africa* (New York: Women's Refugee Commission, 2013), 3, at: https://www.womensrefugeecommission.org/images/zdocs/Our_Motherland,_Our_Country_final_for_web.pdf.

11.   UNHCR, "Preventing Statelessness: Southeast Asian Countries Share Lessons," UNHRC website, 29 October 2010, at: http://www.unhcr.org/4ccae1009.html.

12.   See Kitty McKinsey, "Lose a Husband, Lose a Country," *Refugees Magazine* 147: 3 (2007), 26-27, at: http://www.unhcr.org/46d2e8dc2.html.

13.   See Mark Manly, "Sorry, Wrong Gender," *Refugees Magazine* 147:3 (2007), 25, at: http://www.unhcr.org/46d2e8dc2.html.

14.   UNHCR, *Removing Gender Discrimination from Nationality Laws*, Campaign to End Statelessness within 10 years, Good Practice Paper Action 3, 3, at: http://www.refworld.org/pdfid/54f8377d4.pdf.

Chapter 3: Stateless Children

1.   UNHCR, *I Am Here, I Belong: The Urgent Need to Address Childhood Statelessness* (UNHCR, Division of International Protection, 2015), 1, at: http://www.unhcr.org/ibelong/wp-content/uploads/2015-10-StatelessReport_ENG16.pdf.

2.   Ibid., 6.

3.   Ibid., 9.

4.   Ibid., 19.

5.   Ibid., 18.

6.   UNHCR, *Guidelines on Statelessness no. 4: Ensuring Every Child's Right to Acquire a Nationality through Articles 1-4 of the 1961 Convention on the Reduction of Statelessness*, UNHCR, HCR/GS/12/04 (21 December 2012), 2, at: http://www.refworld.org/docid/50d460c72.html.

7.   UN General Assembly, *Birth Registration and the Right of Everyone to Recognition Everywhere as a Person Before the Law*, Human Rights Council 27th Session, UN General Assembly, A/HRC/27/22, 17 June 2014, 3.

8.   UNICEF, *A Passport to Protection: A Guide to Birth Registration Programming* (UNICEF, 2013), 28, at: http://www.unicef.org/protection/files/UNICEF_Birth_Registration_Handbook.pdf.

9.   UNICEF, *Every Child's Birth Right: Inequities and Trends in Birth Registration* (UNICEF, 2013), 15, at: http://www.unicef.org/media/files/Embargoed_11_Dec_Birth_Registration_report_low_res.pdf

10.   UNICEF, *Factsheet: Birth Registration*, Press Centre, UNICEF website, at: http://www.unicef.org/newsline/2003/03fsbirthregistration.htm

11.   "Tanzania Rolls out Birth Registration by Mobile Phone," Al Jazeera, 14 October 2015, at: http://www.aljazeera.com/news/2015/10/tanzania-rolls-birth-registration-mobile-phone-151014134550042.html.

12.   UN General Assembly, *Birth Registration and the Right*, 7.

13.   UNICEF, "Child Marriage," UNICEF website, 22 October 2014, at: http://www.unicef.org/protection/57929_58008.html.

14.　See Maureen Lynch and Melanie Teff, "Childhood Statelessness," *Forced Migration Review* 32 (April 2009), 32.

15.　See Sarnata Reynolds and Daryl Grisgraber, "Birth Registration in Turkey: Protecting the Future for Syrian Children," Refugees International, Field Report (30 April 2015), 4.

Chapter 4: Statelessness and Displacement

1.　UNHCR, *Two Camps of Thought on Helping Rohingya in Bangladesh*, UNHCR website (28 January 2013), at: http://www.unhcr.org/5106a7609.html.

2.　Human Rights Watch, "Background: History of the Rohinga People," HRW website, at: https://www.hrw.org/reports/2000/malaysia/maybr008-01.htm.

3.　Human Rights Watch, Dominican Republic: Thousands at Risk of Expulsion to Haiti, HRW website, 30 June 2015, at: https://www.hrw.org/news/2015/06/30/dominican-republic-thousands-risk-expulsion-haiti.

4.　See Michele Wucker, "The Dominican Republic's Shameful Deportation Legacy," *Foreign Policy*, 8 October 2015, at: http://foreignpolicy.com/2015/10/08/dominican-republic-haiti-trujillo-immigration-deportation/

5.　Zahra Albarazi and Laura van Waas, *Statelessness and Displacement: Scoping Paper* (Norwegian Refugee Council, 2015), 17.

6.　Ibid., 23.

7.　For example, Jane McAdam, *Climate Change Displacement and International Law: Complementary Protection Standards*, UNHCR, Legal and Protection Policy Research Series, May 2011, at: http://www.unhcr.org/4dff16e99.pdf.

8.　Susin Park, *Climate Change and the Risk of Statelessness: The Situation of Low-lying Island States*, UNHCR, Legal and Protection Policy Research Series, May 2011, 18.

9.   European Network on Statelessness, *Protecting Stateless Persons from Arbitrary Detention: A Regional Toolkit for Practitioners*, December 2015, 3, at: http://www.statelessness.eu/sites/www.statelessness.eu/files/ENS_Detention_Toolkit.pdf.

10.   *Belonging, Part One*, YouTube video, Lee Dourens, at: https://www.youtube.com/watch?v=s07egavs3FM.

11.   Equal Rights Trust, *ERT Guidelines to Protect Stateless Persons from Arbitrary Detention* (2012), Guidline 41, 22.

12.   See Katherine Perks and Jarlath Clifford, "The Legal Limbo of Detention," *Forced Migration Review* 32 (April 2009), 42.

13.   UN Office on Drugs and Crime, *United Nations Convention against Transnational Organized Crime and the Protocols Thereto* (New York: United Nations, 2014), 42, at: https://www.unodc.org/documents/treaties/UNTOC/Publications/TOC%20Convention/TOCebook-e.pdf.

14.   Human Rights Watch, "Thailand: Mass Graves of Rohingya Found in Trafficking Camp," HRW website, 1 May 2015, at: https://www.hrw.org/news/2015/05/01/thailand-mass-graves-rohingya-found-trafficking-camp.

15.   WCC, *Statement on the Human Rights of Stateless People* (WCC, 8 November 2013), at: https://www.oikoumene.org/en/resources/documents/assembly/2013-busan/adopted-documents-statements/human-rights-of-stateless-people.

Chapter 5: The Way Forward

1.   See Bishop Duleep de Chickera, "Journeying with the God of Life," in *Encountering the God of Life*, ed. Erlinda N. Senturias and Theodore A. Gill, Jr. (Geneva: WCC Publications, 2014), 61.

2.   WCC, *Christian Perspectives on Theological Anthropology*, Faith and Order Paper 199 (Geneva: WCC Publications, 2005), 14.

3.   WCC, *The Church: Towards a Common Vision*, Faith and Order Paper no. 214, (Geneva: WCC Publications, 2013), 36.

4.   WCC, *Statement on the Human Rights of Stateless People* (WCC, 8 November 2013), at: https://www.oikoumene.org/en/resources/documents/assembly/2013-busan/adopted-documents-statements/human-rights-ofstateless-people.

5.   WCC, *The Church: Towards a Common Vision.*

6.   See Olav F. Tveit, "The Pilgrimage of Justice and Peace," *Ecumenical Review* 66:2 (July 2014), 127.

7.   *An Invitation to the Pilgrimage of Justice and Peace*, WCC Central Committee, Geneva, 8 July 2014, at: http://www.oikoumene.org/en/resources/documents/central-committee/geneva-2014/an-invitation-to-the-pilgrimage-of-justice-and-peace.

8.   Ibid.

9.   Ibid.

10.   Ibid.

11.   UNCHR, *2014-24 Global Action Plan to End Statelessness* (UNHCR, Division of International Protection, 2014), at: http://www.unhcr.org/statelesscampaign2014/Global-Action-Plan-eng.pdf.

12.   WCC, *Religious Plurality and Christian Self-Understanding*, Preparatory and Background Document for the WCC 9th Assembly, Porto Alegre, 14 February 2006.

13.   WCC, *Den Dolder Recommendations* (14 September 2014), at: http://www.oikoumene.org/en/press-centre/files/DENDOLDERREC-OMMENDATIONS.pdf.

14.   UN, *Transforming Our World: The 2030 Agenda for Sustainable Development*, A/RES/70/1 (United Nations, 2015), 1, at: https://sustainabledevelopment.un.org/content/documents/21252030%20Agenda%20for%20Sustainable%20Development%20web.pdf.

15.   Amal DeChickera, *Statelessness, Human Rights and Development: It's Time to Connect the Dots*, European Network on Statelessness blog (8 October 2013), at: http://www.statelessness.eu/blog/statelessness-human-rights-and-development-its-time-connect-dots.

16. UN, *Transforming Our World*, 5.

17. Ibid., 27.

18. Marc de Boni, "Que deviennent les apatrides," *Slate*, 11 August 2010, http://www.slate.fr/story/25981/apatrides-decheance-nationalite.

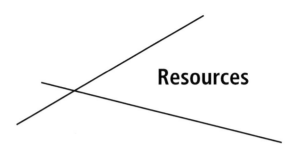

Resources

Recommended reading

Nationality and Statelessness under International Law, edited by Alice Edwards and Laura van Waas, Cambridge University Press, 2014

Nationality and Statelessness: A Handbook for Parliamentarians, United Nations High Commissioner for Refugees and Inter-Parliamentary Union, 20 October 2005

Global Action Plan to End Statelessness, United Nations High Commissioner for Refugees, 4 November 2014

I Am Here, I Belong: The Urgent Need to End Childhood Statelessness, United Nations High Commissioner for Refugees, 3 November 2015

The Origins of Totalitarianism, Hannah Arendt, revised ed.,New York: Schocken, 2004 [1951]

Recommended video resources

I Belong: End Statelessness Now, United Nations High Commissioner for Refugees (UNHCR)
https://www.youtube.com/watch?v=X2opUDSVXns

Living as a Stateless Person, Australia for UNHCR
https://www.youtube.com/watch?v=iQ9SzaumyW0

Statelessness in Lebanon: Leal's Story, UNHCR
https://www.youtube.com/watch?v=XG0BRvulTAo

No Nationality, No Rights: Stateless People in the Dominican Republic,
Amnesty International
https://www.youtube.com/watch?v=jw-_TN0TJoI

Stateless, Open Society Foundation
https://www.youtube.com/watch?v=poCUxsduHM4